LEADING ME

Becoming My Life's CEO

Dr. Ndidi Precious Alino

LEADING ME: Becoming My Life's CEO
Copyright © 2021 by Dr. Ndidi Precious Alino
All rights reserved. No part of this book may be reproduced, duplicated, or transmitted in any form or by any means without the prior written permission of the author.

Disclaimer: This is a work of nonfiction and reflects the author's unique experiences, opinions, and ideas. Certain names and characteristics may have been withheld. Some events have been compressed or recreated to fit the purpose of the book. The ideas and strategies outlined in this book may not work for everyone in every situation. The author disclaims any liability that results from applying these strategies.

ISBN 978-1-7363532-0-2
Printed in the United States of America
By Amazon KDP Print

For all enquiries, contact the author at:
www.credablemindset.com

Cover Design by Jahn Ade Creative Designs
Cover Photo by Olunife Ofomata

Dedication

This book is dedicated to the loving memory of my late sister, Mrs. Ngozi Chinyere Okeke (née Ezekwe). You never stopped living in the minds of your loved ones.

Acknowledgment

With special gratitude to the Almighty God from whom all blessings flow. Thank you, Lord, for your unfailing love, mercy, and bountiful grace that makes all things possible, including providing me with the strength, time, inspiration, wisdom, and knowledge that brought this book to fruition.

To my parents Rev (Mr.) George Ezekwe & Mrs. Paulina Ezekwe, and my siblings for providing the unwavering foundation on which my success stories rest upon. I am grateful for your unconditional love, prayers, and support in every aspect of the word support. I couldn't have asked for a better family to be born and raised in. I consider myself blessed to be part of this bloodline.

To my darling husband, Mr. Henry Alino, who always believes in me and encourages me to explore my talents. Your love and support have helped me to see windows of opportunities and to explore all possibilities. You are simply amazing, and I cannot thank you enough.

To my four bundles of joy; my awesomely gifted children, Prince, Favour, Kingsley, and Royal. You are a divine bundle of inspiration, and my life would have been so incomplete without every single one of you. You inspire me to do more, live more, and leave the right footsteps.

How can I forget you, my amazing friends and cheerleaders, mentors, heroes, spiritual pillars, and everyone who has inspired me in one way or another; thank you for your support and encouragement. Some of you never stopped checking on me to know how far I have gone with this book. Thank you for helping me stay motivated. A special thanks to Bukola Somide for providing me with some guidance on the self-publishing process.

I am particularly thankful to Olunife Ofomata for always making sure I am on the right social media platforms. Thank you for your marketing insights; this book will not be complete without a note of thanks to you.

Finally, I want to thank you, the reader, for buying this book and making my effort worthwhile. I am grateful for your time and money that you have invested in my work.

Author's Quote

If you can commit to making a better YOU each day, an incredible YOU will definitely emerge over time.

Table of Contents

Dedication
Acknowledgment
Author's Quote
Foreword
Preface
Introduction
Chapter 1: Scripting My Life's Blank Pages
Chapter 2: Dream it, Believe it, Make it Happen
Chapter 3: Love the Person in the Mirror
Chapter 4: The Influences that Make Us
Chapter 5: The Good Outlier
Chapter 6: Push the Limits
Chapter 7: A Legacy that Lasts
About the Author
Bonus: Other Works by the Author

Foreword

Is it possible to be Martha and Mary at the same time?
In Luke 10:38-42, Martha was busy serving, while Mary sat at Jesus' feet. I used to think that it was not possible until I met Dr. Ndidi Precious Alino.

Dr. P, like myself and many in her inner circle affectionately call her, has a servant heart, a gift of hospitality, an extraordinary work ethic, and a worship mantle. All while executing each part of her life with flawless ease and grace that is breathtaking to behold.

On May 22, 2020; *her* birthday, my dear soul sister and friend asked me to pen the foreword to this book. I told Dr. P that she had just given *me* the gift of a lifetime and for that, I am deeply honored and humbled. Almost a year earlier during my birthday month in February 2019, Dr. P first told me that she was writing a book. She mentioned that she started the early workings of the book from several notes she had jotted down in her diary. She also discussed her non-profit organization she wanted to start, Diamond Sister International Elite Club, to help leaders build each other up and mentor the next generation to achieve success and greatness. A few months later, she established that non-profit and asked me to be the Vice President, which I humbly accepted. From that point until now, Dr. P has periodically shared deeper insights into this book while we brainstormed on goals for the new non-profit.

Dr. Ndidi Precious Alino is an accomplished Pharmacy Director at one of the top hospitals in Arizona. She has taught university courses, leads the youth group at the church we both attend, while also serving as a praise team member. A mother of four and a doting wife, I admire her faithfulness to her commitments, her grit, and her tenacity to accomplish the goals she sets for herself all while still taking the time to be present for others.

As highly accomplished and immensely busy as she is, she makes space for those that otherwise feel left out or ignored. I can honestly say I have been one of those people at times, but never in the presence of Dr. P., her nature is attentive, loving, and caring. A truly beautiful person inside and out.

There are very few people in this world that can understand the magnitude of the assignment

God has given each of us. When you can see that in each other, that is a treasure that cannot be thrown away or taken for granted. Again, I can say that in Dr. P, I have found the one.

Yes, Dr. P has a tremendous amount of personal and professional accomplishments. However, in this book, *Leading Me: Becoming My Life's CEO*, she is not telling you how to be like her, but how to be truly YOU. Make no assumptions about this book before you read it. Read it with an open mind and heart. Let it penetrate the deepest parts of you so you will be able to gain the most out of it. As the book's title alludes to, it is your time to lead you. As Dr. P will share with you through her own life's mastery and wisdom, it is time to be your life's CEO.

Foreword by
Olunife Ofomata
Founder & CEO, Sweeter Juice Beauty
Vice President, DSI Elite Club

Preface

LEADING ME is a personal leadership book inspired by everyday personal life experiences and interactions with people from all works of life. I often encounter some young people who dress up in an almost indecent and questionable manner, not because it is a true representation of who they are, rather, they just want to please their friends and other kids in school to avoid being ridiculed. My 16-year-old teenage son once said (about two years ago), "I don't want that haircut! Please don't do that to me!" "If I wear that, or look like that, I will be an object of ridicule in school," and so on. As I sat down there and listened to him lament about my style suggestion for his haircut, I could not help but wonder how many times I have let others decide how I am supposed to look. It is usually about the trend and what everyone else thinks. I recall a brief conversation I had with a young man back in the days at the university, whose pants are almost dropping to the floor and he constantly struggles every other minute to pull it up to his waist as it drops to his knees. It was hard for me to ignore this, so I could not help but ask him politely if he was enjoying this overly inconvenient outlook, as I walked past him. He looked at me, smiled, and said, "miss, that's what's up." Then, I replied, I think it is overly inconvenient and does not appear so fancy for all the trouble. Almost two weeks after, someone walks up and taps me on the shoulder from behind as I was hurrying to the student parking garage and says, "miss, I am wearing a belt today and I thought I should have you see my new look." Honestly, I did not recognize him, (it has been a couple of weeks since I spoke to him and I did not pay too much attention to his face at the time, so he had to remind me how I stopped him and spoke to him about his sagging pants). I asked him if he liked his new look and he said, "I won't lie, it feels much better." Notice that his response to me about his sagging pants earlier has nothing to do with his personal choice and interest. It is more about what he thinks is the acceptable outlook according to his social group and natural influencers.

  As I continued the walk to my car, I wondered how many more people are inconveniencing themselves just to maintain the "what's up" or should I say everyone else's standard. A standard that we neither know the originator nor the purpose behind it. A standard that hardly represents who we are within. Instead, we commit to living a life where we are constantly waiting to be validated by the world around us. Permit me to say that you may have to wait for eternity if you are waiting to be validated by all, especially if your move is an unpopular one. We live a life where we are either living up to the expectations of a constantly changing and demanding world, or one where we are so stressed out from such demands that we eventually succumb to self-pity and play the blame game. I am not sure which of the two lives you are living now, but either of the two lives is pitiful. Hence the need for a life where you can take back control and lead the course.

This book is intended to give back the steering wheel to the original owner. One that understands his/her life's purpose and willing to drive it to the finish line. This life has been given to you and there is nothing wrong with putting in some intentional work into living it right.

I have served in a few leadership roles between my career and other professional/charitable affiliations, but I am yet to see people in leadership positions give enough attention and effort in leading the many aspects of their individual lives. There is usually an overwhelming imbalance between the time allotted to other things outside of our personal lives than what our life and emotions can tolerate. We put in overtime in these exuberant careers while fitting the rest of our aspirations around whatever is left of our zeal and energy.

This piece is written with you in mind: be you a teenager, young adult, my running mates in their fabulous forties, not to forget those of you in your fancy fifties, and of course, the celebrated sixties, seventies, and beyond. Believe it or not, regardless of your age, life experiences, and personal achievements, there is one chapter or two in this book just for you. It is never too late, neither is it ever too early to take the lead over your life. I am sure you may have heard the saying that, "today is the beginning of the rest of your life."

You cannot afford to continue giving your life just a mere fraction of your God-given potential. Every individual is uniquely endowed with a special deposit of potential that ought to be maximized. Sometimes we make the mistake of focusing on what the world wants from us, that we fail to pay attention to what our life is expecting from us. Every single day of your life eagerly awaits your attention and hopes each day that it is not faced with disappointment. You cannot disappoint TODAY because you think YESTERDAY was great and as such, should be enough. Neither can you ignore TOMORROW because TODAY failed to yield much. Your life expects much better from you, and until you can stop and pay attention to every moment of it, it will be impossible to lead it right. Each day is new, different, and special, and therefore deserves its unique attention.

Whether you are looking for daily directions or inspirations, motivations for your dreams, not sure what each day's outcome should be, don't see anything good about you, or you are so well accomplished but not sure whether you are leaving the right legacy behind, there is something in this book for you. Therefore, let this book encourage and invigorate you to not only LEAD YOU but to LEAD YOU right.

Introduction

First, I want to thank you for purchasing this book. Thank you for making it worth the effort. By the way, if you are on this page, that means you are a detail-oriented individual who takes the time to read the introductory part of a book. I am also glad that this is not just another collection to beautify your bookshelf. So, I want to say thank you! If you are not a voracious reader, that means you consciously make a selection of what to read, then, it is safe to say that one of the reasons you bought this book is not only to support the author but to lead your life right. So, I must congratulate you on one more step in the right direction.

I often consider my life an adventure packaged in a book with several pages that make up the chapters. A book that is so voluminous and overly complex that it is often hard to determine where the author is taking me to next. I just know that I must act a particular script each day. I am in a movie every minute of the day from the moment I was born through the rest of my life. Wow! I am a movie star! Except I don't get paid for it. The interesting aspect of this adventure-packed script called life is that some of it has been defined and written without my permission. However, what I failed to recognize initially is that I am a co-author of this storybook.

To me, life is a story. A story better told by me, so I want to take the lead in the acting and narrating of the story. I want to play the lead role, after all, it is my life's script. The story of how I just opened my tiny little eyes one day to behold the light of the world and the warm embrace of a grateful mother and a half-written book with several empty pages was handed to me. Like you, I may not like the introductory section of this storybook; the setting, and the other characters mentioned in the beginning chapter of my life's book. For instance, I was not granted the opportunity to choose my place of birth, and neither did anyone consult me before making that choice for me. Nobody even asked my opinion about the choice of breast milk over formula, or if I wanted a combination of both. Can you even imagine that! Those are choices I could not make for sure. I did not have a choice about who my parents, or siblings are. Fortunately for me, I fell in love with them at the first glance and I was just happy for that choice. My point is this, I did not have a choice about so many things in this first chapter of my life, including my skin color, my race, and socioeconomic background at birth. These pages and chapters have already been written. I call it the chapter "ONE" of my life. Nobody gets the chance to write the beginning chapter of their life. It is written and done, so any time spent on regrets concerning your first chapter is an absolute waste! Unfortunately, most of what hold people back from fulfilling their destiny always go back to the enduring regrets of whatever was not done right in the initial chapter. The good news is that there are so many more pages and chapters that are yet unwritten, and that has accorded me the opportunity to author this book.

    This book is intended to be a living breathing guide to writing the rest of your story. It accords me the pleasure of being the CEO of the most complex organization there is, ME! So why spend my energy worrying about the initial chapter of my life that is already written, the things I cannot change? I, therefore, decided to focus my energy on what I know, what I believe in, and what I can change. I can define and influence the subsequent chapters of this storybook called ME. I am the lead character, so I intend to give my life's movie my best shot! Another interesting aspect of my life's storybook is that I can customize it to reflect my life's purpose, goals, ambitions, and preferences. It is my life, it is my course, so I am going to lead it. I am not hiring another CEO over my life!

Therefore, every chapter of this book is meant to guide you towards leading your life as you would expect the best-trained CEO to lead an effective and efficient organization. Starting from scripting your life's blank pages, loving who you are, and paying attention to the influences within and around you, to living your dreams and building a lasting legacy. The various stories and examples are meant to inspire and motivate you to lead your course in your unique way. The stories are your steering wheel to drive you, but the navigation system is ultimately yours. I implore you to let the chapters enliven you and you will be amazed at how much strength you have within. Hopefully, this book helps you to find right within you, the strength to strive, conquer and most importantly, lead the most complicated organization there is, YOU!

LEADING ME

Chapter 1

Scripting My Life's Blank Pages

Chapter Highlight
Don't live your life like a blank sheet of paper waiting to be written on by everyone else but yourself.

Life does not necessarily come with a manual. Even your biological parents are yet to figure you out. Sometimes you are in utter bewilderment as to why you still can't do certain things right and unable to fathom why you keep making mistakes after mistakes. Let's face the fact; the truth is, we are all trying to figure life out. One good thing that life provides us is a blank slate with each sunrise and sunset that we are privileged to see. So why not start with your very own personalized script.

Life is an ongoing movie, and you are your life's best scriptwriter. Writing your life's script requires focus, planning, and series of actions while leaving room for little or no distractions. Think about the movies and television dramas that come in several episodes within the seasons, where the writers and the producers are orchestrating the characters' daily actions. They work on each scene in advance; otherwise, the characters will run out of action. The characters are depending on the scriptwriters for every action they need to take. In the same manner, your life is waiting on you for daily directions. In your hand is the prospect to make the best movie there is about YOU, but it does not come without preparation, discipline, determination, and action.

While in Pharmacy school, we had an instructor who would ask questions to determine if we studied before coming to class. If this instructor does not get a good response from the students (which happens quite often), then the next thing we hear is, "don't come here like a blank sheet of paper saying write on me." It was not a statement we wanted to hear because all we can think of is how busy we are with other competing priorities. We often wondered why this instructor could not see that we have other things going on besides this one class. Neither were we so thrilled with hearing the same speech repeatedly, let alone when someone refers to you as a blank sheet of paper. As a result, we will always complete the statement once we hear the first two words, mainly to deflate the seriousness of whatever is being said.

Interestingly, I was in a meeting several years after, where we observed a vendor demonstration of a new device that is supposed to provide an additional safety net while also increasing efficiency for the users. I cannot remember who the vendor is or the product under review, but it must have been a boring presentation because most people in the room were busy doodling on the papers in front of them. I was alarmed to see different representations of shapes and figures on the notepads in front of each person that was once blank but now filled with meaningless drawings. It became apparent what it means to be a blank sheet of paper and the vulnerability of blank slates. These papers were supposed to be used for taking notes that will become a reference point for making final considerations about the product. However, there was nothing about the product on these papers. Right there, at that moment, I started to think about life in general and how often we may present ourselves as blank slates without even realizing it.

Every single day of your life represents several pages of unwritten words, and these pages become a perfect canvas for other people to use for both meaningful and irrelevant expressions. A blank slate can only hope that it ends up in the hands of a great artist who will use it to capture the perfect or intended image. The bad news is that not all blank slates end up in the hands of great artists. It is also possible that the blank slate could end up in the hands of the world's greatest artist, but the final product is highly dependent on the artist's mood at that time, so the end product could be far from what is anticipated. Sometimes, it is hard to understand what the artist is trying to portray, so it is left to everyone's interpretation. I am sure you may have come across such paintings at some point.

My biggest fear and potential disappointment in life is mainly not the fact that it is possible to come close to the end of my life, only to realize that I have several blank pages. While I hope that is not the case, my worst fear is to have these pages filled by other people, with things that hardly represent who I am and what I stand for, simply because I provided them the perfect slates. This chapter focuses on helping you realize that even though you may not be able to rewrite history, your life, however it is today, represent millions of blank pages that require your undivided attention. You can embody your life's purpose on these blank pages each day. So, rather than dwell on the regrets of yesterday, pick up your pen each day and script your life's controllable activities. These blank pages are the scripts you must act each day, and they need to be carefully outlined because there is an expected action for every moment of your life. You are your scriptwriter as well as the actor or actress. The pages are endless; they are as many as the number of days you have left to live. You have a lot to write, so flip through the pages and let's make this adventure, called life, a successful and remarkable one together.

What you write is as significant as scripting your blank pages. In fact, what you write, is even more imperative. Recognize that the title of this chapter is not "filling my life's blank pages" but "scripting my life's blank pages." You do not just fill the pages or write for the sake of writing; the pages should reflect your life's purpose, passions, expectations, hopes, dreams, strategic steps, as well as anticipated positive outcomes. Therefore, you should not leave any page blank because you cannot guarantee that any other person writing on it will be representing your interest.

It will be a fundamental error to write a book on how to lead your life successfully without addressing the importance of recognizing your life's purpose. Your life's purpose is the genesis of who you are, and therefore should be carefully scripted on your life's blank pages. Living without purpose is like living a borrowed life. If you do not have a clear comprehension of what your life's purpose is, you could be in a constant struggle trying to live some other person's life, which is a life you are not equipped for. Meanwhile, you are creating a big vacuum in the world because your unique function is left unattended and unfulfilled.

Chapter Highlight
Make every effort to be on your daily scheduled path just like the school bus.

Several individuals have tried to define life's purpose or attempted to guide people towards purposeful living but have often erroneously narrowed it down to the individual's dreams, goals, and ambitions. The truth is that your life's purpose does not start and end with you. It is mostly not about you and what you want. You need to spend some time to personally understand why you are here on earth. This is important, especially during depressing moments when harmful thoughts creep in, because it will be selfish to take a life that will create a negative chain reaction in other people's lives. Part of the journey to discovering your life's purpose is to recognize that there are so many people that have been placed on your path each day, whose success in life is dependent on your ability to be on your scheduled route and at the right time. Not only are you expected to be purposeful, but also supposed to be sensitive to the demands of time and space. If you are expected to be on a certain path on a Tuesday, you can't just negligently show up on a Friday or two months after. The opportunity that is available on Tuesday may not be there on Friday. Therefore, you must lead yourself accordingly by being on that unique path on the right day and at the specified time, to lead others right. Life is intertwined in series of events, and there are several lives attached to your success that will be negatively impacted by your undue failures. This is not only about the other lives that are attached to your success, being at the right place at the right time often results in life-transforming breakthroughs for individuals who are astute enough to make their schedule and diligent enough to keep the agenda of the day.

  I am not in any way saying that failure is unexpected throughout your personal leadership journey. It is okay to express doubts and fears, but with recognizable approaches to overcome such negative expressions. Each day of your life presents you with an entirely new page, and what you put down on that page makes a lot of difference in the outcomes of the day. You have three options, to leave the page blank, print some positive declarations, or fill the page with negative statements. You also have the opportunity to strike through pages from yesterday that have the wrong expressions or representations. The choice is yours, but I hope that you are not leaving blank pages for others to write on them for you. I say this because if you refuse to write on these blank pages, some other person or persons will write on them. If the latter is the case, then, you may just have to live the rest of your life based on a script written by people who may not have your best interest at heart. Whatever you do, never leave your page blank, because it is an act of carelessness and irresponsibility. I believe that enough has been written for you already by nature. This chapter intends that you pick up from where nature and other uncontrollable authors have left and chart the remaining course of your life.

I would therefore like to spend some time to discuss the importance of focusing on what you write and the types of statements you make on each page of your life's storybook. This is important because your expectations go a long way in influencing your outcomes. You may not be able to control certain situations that arise each day, the daily disappointments and failures that may redirect your path to where you never intended to head to in the first place. Yes, you cannot control the tides and waves of life. You may not even know when the tides will come, and neither do you know when fortunes will come knocking. One thing you know when it comes is the statements and declarations you make and the strategic steps you take towards success. That being said, you should focus more of your energy and time on what brings value to your life and the lives of others around you. You must wake up every single day with expectations, whether it be the unfulfilled expectations of yesterday or new expectations for the day. You cannot just wake up for the sake of waking up without goals and expectations, especially when there are people whose lives are hanging on the balance with life support devices and machinery hoping to wake up. Each day you wake up deserves its chance. So, please don't waste any day. Why not make bold and confident statements each day and work towards bringing them to fruition? Why not translate all your dreams into a breathing script fueled by action?

    Fortunately, I am a practicing Christian, hence, it is even more critical that I pay attention to what I say and write over my life. It is also very imperative that I mind what others speak over my life and make corrective statements whenever necessary. Each day of your life is as significant as the day you were born, so when people make false and negative statements over your life, you ought to declare and write the correct version as quickly as possible before it becomes an indelible ink. You should not become an average student because your teacher, friend, or even parent(s) said so. You only become an average student or person when you say or believe so. Likewise, you do not operate below your standard just because the world wants you to be so. Often, we are worth more than what others can ever imagine.

  Each person is like a work of art; no matter how incredible the artist thinks you are, people will still view and interpret you from so many different perspectives. It does not matter what their interpretation is, and you should not waste time trying to change their mind. You should focus on your understanding of who you are and how incredible your designer thinks you are. Have you wondered why people will often say to you, "oh, wow! I didn't realize you can do that." They say that because you are viewed from a different perspective each time by different people. Some people may look at you and conclude that you are empty-headed even before you utter a word. When someone says you are an average person, that does not make you an average person; you only become mediocre when you accept it and eventually start acting like one. Even people who are very close to you, who may know you well, could still have so many things wrong about you, if they are to write your life's script, except they ask for clarifications. One good example is this game that is often played at bridal showers or the newlywed games, where each partner is to answer specific questions about their spouse. Have you noticed how many times these partners get the answers wrong even though they are supposed to know each other well? Take shoe sizes, for instance; I have had a few people who are close to me express some surprise about my shoe size almost every time. Funny enough, when I asked them to say what size they think I wear, they were almost always saying sizes 8 or 8.5. We have natural assumptions about other people based on certain factors, and those assumptions may not be accurate. My example above is a very harmless assumption that may not have a negative consequence. Certain assumptions of other people about you can result in negative consequences if you allow it to become how you view yourself. I will not buy a size 8 or 8.5 pair of shoes just because most people think that it is the appropriate size for me when my actual size is 9.5 (well, now you know).

If I will not accept their assumption and cut one or two inches from my toes or heel just to fit into their assumption of my shoe size, why should I then try to fit into their unexceptional assumption of me if I know I can do better? Why should I then give up my dreams because someone thinks it will not be successful, or that I don't have what it takes? It is important to recognize that people often have a certain image of what a smart, beautiful, or successful person should look like, so if you don't fit into that preconceived image, you are miscategorized. Hopefully, you are beginning to imagine the number of errors that could be on your life's script if it were to be written by other people. Therefore, your life's agenda is best written by you because you are the only one that truly knows who you are and what you are capable of doing.

  Several years ago, when I was in the 9th grade in an all-girls high school back in Nigeria, we were getting ready for what we called an interhouse sports competition. There were four Houses identified by the colors Blue, Green, Red, and Yellow, and each girl was assigned to one of these Houses led by a House Captain (a Senior) and a Housemistress (a teacher). I was assigned to Yellow House (I have entirely forgotten the school's process for the selection). However, I remember that I was happy to be in Yellow House. Our House captain was the tallest student in the school, very beautiful, and a nationally recognized sports icon, especially in the games of volleyball and girls' basketball. You can imagine what it feels like to be on this team. I was very slender at that time, pretty (they said), and have runners' legs, according to them. Both the Housemistress and the House captain were excited that I was on their team. So, they hoped I would do the 100 meters and 200 meters race for the House. Imagine their disappointment when I told them that I don't run. I informed them that such fast-paced running gives me a headache, as a matter of fact! What a waste and disappointment, I am sure they muttered within. Then, they both asked, can you at least be the House Queen and be in front during the marching band parade? In excitement, knowing I can finally be of relevance and contribute to the success of our team, I said, "of course."

People may underestimate or overextend your abilities, or make you believe that you are either completely incompetent or unduly equipped for success. While some individuals are totally comfortable with mediocrity, it is important first to assess and evaluate yourself wholly to discover any hidden potentials before accepting the average standard of life. Being a low performer or less ambitious could mean that you need to analyze your skills and personality traits to recognize if you are in your maximum impact profession, business, or environment. If you are a high performer, this analysis will help you to continuously aim to be an excellent performer rather than the continuous struggle from incompetence to second-rate. Hence, I emphasize the importance of recognizing who you are as a person, identifying your belief system and values, and how these can be translated to a success story. You cannot accept mediocrity until a full assessment is completed, and the outcome, (not mediocrity) should be your script. This will require self-determination and self-motivation, but not without first recognizing that you are doing this for yourself and not to please anyone.

Another reason why you want to mind what you write is that this is not some fairy tale or some fantasy movie script. This script is your life's story; a living breathing movie. Each page should reflect personal abilities, preferences, likes, and dislikes. There should be room for anticipated failures along the way, and you should learn from each failure while providing an avenue to celebrate every success. Each page should also include skills and approaches needed to withstand and overcome temptation. There is a need to recognize the different sources of negative influences and implement plans to overcome such forces. Not only are you expected to outline the goals and objectives for each day, but you are also expected to provide adequate time and resources necessary to accomplish these goals. Otherwise, you will become more familiar with the word failure.

Finally, page after page should reflect the fact that you are learning from the mistakes of yesterday while staying present enough for the day at hand. Learning and growing from your mistakes requires courage, patience, and humility. It requires that you recognize the difference between your goals and daily distractions. It also requires that you make room for humor and relaxation. Think about each page as an improvement process. If there is no improvement from failures recorded on previous pages, you may be moving in the wrong direction. Each new page should present better strategies that stem from mistakes and successes of preceding pages. It will be the highest height of self-deceit to expect a better outcome if you do the same things wrong and carry them on from page to page, from day to day, and from year to year. I encourage you to assess and understand the underlying reason or reasons behind every success, as well as every failure. These reasons are important factors that determine whether you will replicate successes or failures. I don't know about you, but I will rather replicate successes, therefore, I encourage you to write these reasons down in preparation for the next chapters of your life, the other blank pages. What you write on each page matters and should inform the next page!

Table 1: Factors that contribute to blank pages. Watch out for some of these pointers and redirect your steps as quickly as possible.

Lack of vision	There is no sense of direction, so anything goes. "Where there is no vision, the people perish." – Prov 29:18
Action deficiency syndrome	This is the most painful in my opinion because you don't want others to write on you, yet your lack of action provides the perfect canvas for them. You have the knowledge and the vision, but you just cannot act, probably due to self-doubt, lack of drive, or possibly due to insufficient zeal. You are waiting to be validated. You just cannot find the right time to act.
Indifference	You could care less. Not only are you saying, "write on me," the indifferent attitude also means "I don't care what you write on me."
Luke-warmness	When you are luke-warm, you are neither here nor there, and you are basically leaving your life up for

	grabs by either the sweltering people or the frigid individuals. You are in a state of confusion and not sure where you belong.
Procrastination	You find yourself always postponing tasks. You will instead do it any other time, as long as it is not at the present time. You could miss out on some growth opportunities and possible success stories as a result.
Self-doubt	You never believe you can do anything or do it right, so you refuse to try. Sometimes it is because of the influence of people on you. Other times, it is just because you've never really accomplished any significant thing in your life, so you are afraid to push yourself any further. You focus more on the many reasons why you are incapable more than you think of your potentials and unique qualities.
Self-pity	This is self-doubt justified. Not only are you always rationalizing

your incapability, but you also always want to draw sympathy to yourself at any given opportunity. All you see are your extenuating circumstances and qualifying reasons why your predicament must be understood and acknowledged. The problem with self-pity is that you are left at the mercy of other people's comfort. You are always waiting for people to recognize your pain and sympathize with your plight. Your drive is dependent on people's acknowledgment of your pain and difficulty. When you fail to get such acknowledgment, it eventually leads to a state of helplessness and hopelessness.

Consider seeking help from a professional life coach if one or more of these pointers become a pattern.

Chapter 2

Dream It, Believe It, Make It Happen

<u>Chapter Highlight</u>
It is only natural for people to tell you what they think you can and cannot do. For all the CANNOT, look for one CAN (which is yours) and run with it. Your "CAN" is all you need.

We all have dreams and ambitions, big or small. Some people lack the courage to pursue their dreams; they doubt their strength and fail to attempt. For these set of people, their aspirations, as exciting as it may be, only enjoyed the luxury of the four chambers of their heart, it was never heard of. In fact, if they were sleeping and find their dream becoming a reality in the dreamland, they will wake up in cold sweats and call it a nightmare. This is because they have already restricted their minds to a certain level of success, and anything beyond that level is overly ambitious and not meant for them. To some others, even closing their eyes and imagining success is a luxury they believe they are not worthy of.

Chapter Highlight
Don't be afraid to dream and DREAM BIG! Explore the possibilities; after all, dream is free.

Yet, there are others who take the extra step by allowing their mind to conceive the dream and nurture it. In fact, they are full of energy when it comes to sharing these dreams and ambitions. Nobody can tell the story better than them. They can imagine the result, but that's where it ends; talks and imaginations. Lastly are the advanced stage dreamers. These set of dreamers are very sure of their dream, have set the ball rolling, and have strategically positioned themselves for great achievement. However, they are discouraged due to problems and oppositions. The zeal is not lacking, and the enthusiasm is impressive, but they lack the endurance necessary to overcome obstacles that eventually surface along the way. This chapter, therefore, will not only encourage each set of dreamers but also suggest how to stay focused on your dream and make it a reality irrespective of oppositions.

One thing we all have in common is that we all, at one point or the other feel distressed and have been faced with one tremendous challenge or another. Problems are non-discriminatory. It can present itself to the young or old, rich or poor, smart or dull, tall or short, though with varying magnitude and context. Even the most successful people you can ever think of do have trying moments. What then makes your problems and challenges unique? I guess it is the feeling of guilt, regrets, low personal accomplishment, lack of resilience and the lack of courage to look beyond disappointments. So, even though we all have dreams, what sets each person apart is how each dreamer handles the obstacles along the path that leads to attainment.

Secondly, do not make your problem complex by expecting to get a lot of encouragement from people or to have lots of friends when you are at the bottom of the ladder. People may not want to identify with you at this point. It is almost natural (though not the right thing to do) for people to associate themselves more with smart and successful people. You can minimize your disappointment if you expect less from people and remain focused on your dream journey, especially when you are sitting so low on the ladder of success. Don't expect that most people will buy into your dreams. More so, don't expect that all your friends will buy into it either. Your greatest discouragement might come from people you assume to be your cheerleaders or those you respect so much. You must realize that people discourage you not necessarily because they don't want something good for you, neither is it always that they don't want you to succeed. Often it is because your dream seems overly ambitious to them, and they are advising you from their perspective. Therefore, they are helping you apply brakes where they think your accelerator is moving too fast. However, the resolution to succeed is yours and yours alone. You should not blame them; after all, the vision is yours. These validators you are waiting on do not have the same insight you have, so their mindset have a lot of catching up to do.

    It will also not be of any help to tread the path of self-pity when the outcome of your dream fails to meet your desired expectation. Remember that everyone under the surface of the earth has been unsuccessful in accomplishing one or two things at one point or the other. There is always a story behind the glory, so don't let the resultant success stories of other people deceive you. Sometimes, the failures make the story more beautiful in the end. You may not want to hear this, but the sad reality is that you may not have seen the worst yet. So why let your world come crumbling so soon. It is hard to believe in yourself when you are in a place of self-pity because all you see is somebody that cannot accomplish anything. As a result, you are trying to get people to empathize with you and help you justify your feeling. Do not expect people to believe in you when you do not believe in yourself. You may not have the solution coming fast enough, but trust that one will come.

    Additionally, getting discouraged has never favored anyone, instead have faith in yourself and make optimism a way of life. Learn to avoid the circle where only discouraging words flow. It is very unhealthy. Move with high-spirited people; those that have their eyes set on success no matter how far away it seems to be. Quitting is not an option until all options are exhausted, and trust that there is always one last alternative. A warrior does not conquer by fearing to attack. Recognize that whatever presents itself to you as a challenge today has been tackled by someone, somewhere, and at some point, and their success story is your compelling evidence and proof that you, too, will overcome this challenge one day.

    Maybe you have been deceived in the past to believe that massive dreams and big ambitions are not for you just because of your past mistakes, challenges, or socioeconomic background. Some children who grew up in unstable homes may be able to tell this story better. Possibly an abusive parent or guardian has said to them that they would amount to nothing, yet, some of them ended up growing up to rewrite their stories. Others may have been written off by their grade teacher or college instructor at some point in their academic journey, and they also ended up rewriting the story. These are the advanced-plus dreamers because they did not let minor words of discouragement stop their inner burning desire to succeed. If someone said you would amount to nothing, and you end up becoming nothing, then you have only spent your whole life proving them right. In that case, you have allowed yourself to live up to their expectations of you. You have decided to shut down every word of encouragement and upliftment you have ever received and instead concentrated on the only one that comes with no benefit. You have decided to remember just one "cannot do," or "cannot be" when there may have been several "can be," or "can do" words that have were sent your way numerous times!

While in High school, I had a teacher who joined the school during my 11th-grade year. Part of his teaching portfolio was to make sure we performed exceptionally well in the 12th-grade external exam given to all West African students. He came from the board of education and was an

English Language and Composition instructor. It was made very clear to us upon his hire that his purpose of coming was to prepare us to break the records on this external exam! This instructor believed in every student in the most remarkable way. There were a few students that the other teachers may have considered unserious and intellectually incapable; as a result, these students were not given equal chance and attention. However, to this English Language teacher, everyone deserves a second, third, fourth, and even an endless chance to succeed. He gave everyone equal opportunity and equal attention. His office hours were not just for smart students only; he encouraged and paid genuine attention to every student. Even though I was on the other side with the considerably intelligent and brilliant students, believe it or not (the attention "getters," if you will), I was glad that this teacher was inclusive and gave everyone a chance to live up to their dream. He saw something good in every student, beyond what the other teachers could see. He encouraged and nurtured. Your guess is as good as the outcome; we recorded a remarkable success in that year's exam. It was outstanding!

    I tell this story to let you know that the world is not full of people like my High school English teacher. This means the ball is in your court, and you must play it well, whether your coach believes in you or not. In fact, to effectively take a lead role in your life, you do not need some other person's "can do" for the most part; all you need is just yours. I always say, and I quote myself again, *"It is only natural for people to tell you what they think you can and cannot do. For all the CANNOT, look for one CAN (which is yours) and run with it. Your "CAN" is all you need.*

Therefore, do not give up on your dreams due to discouragements and all the unavoidable waves and tides that life brings your way. There are quite a few positive thinkers and individuals who believe in you and motivate you occasionally. However, do not forget that the same world is full of pessimists, dream killers, and people full of discouraging remarks who do not even know what it means to build anyone up. Do you expect them to magically change because of you and bring you the encouragement you desire? Why then will their opinion matter regarding your dream? You ought to understand that discouragements are not always bad. After all, if we only concentrate on praises and build our world around the accolades we receive from people, it might just become hard to see where improvements are needed. Therefore, be thankful for those who support your dreams and believe in you wholeheartedly while also appreciating the critics and pessimists who see nothing good in your endeavors, as they might just be the catalyst needed to get the best reaction and outcome out of you.

Chapter Highlight
Trials and challenges are the unwanted ingredients that eventually spice up our success stories and the rhythmic sound that attracts the ears to our stories.

Whatever your present circumstance is, it is meant to challenge you to do better and not worse. When you are told repeatedly that you are incapable and unworthy of anything good, the best and ideal comeback is to do everything possible to prove the person wrong. It starts by doing the right things and consequently meeting and working with the right people. Trials and challenges are the unwanted ingredients that eventually spice up our success stories and the rhythmic sound that attracts the ears to our stories. Do not ever forget that!

One major enemy of our would-have-been successful dream is procrastination. Oh! How I wish I have conquered this word in every aspect of my life. I am sure that the problem is not that you don't have good objectives or plans to accomplish your goals. You always almost know the right things to do towards accomplishing your dreams. You also know the right path to take. In fact, you have a mental picture of the rigorous road map as well as the anticipated success super story. You do have the desire to accomplish the set tasks, you even know what to do each day, minute by minute, and yet, you keep pushing it further and further out, day by day. When you think about what you must do, you think about them always in the futuristic state of mind. You hear yourself say things you want to do more in the futuristic state than you ever hear yourself say in the present. We tend to procrastinate more with personal goals because we believe they do not have immediate consequences when the deadline is not met. You are always the last on your calendar and schedule. You fit everybody else on your calendar and then work-around them for your personal goals and dreams.

Chapter Highlight
If you think about it, then do it, don't waste another second thinking about it again.

It is better to visit your future self today if it will help you stop procrastinating and get going on the path to actualizing your dreams. One strategy I employed is to create a personal motivation statement, "if you think about it, then do it, don't waste another second thinking about it again." Have you noticed that we have several creative thinkers, many individuals with brilliant ideas, yet very few people attempt to translate their thoughts to actions? Others do not even have what it takes to generate ideas, but when they get the slightest clue from others, they step into action right away. They don't waste time trying to know if it will work or not. How will you know if it will work when you haven't even tried?

Whenever I drive past a cemetery, I often wonder how many dreams (visions, great ideas, potentials) are buried unfulfilled and unaccomplished because of procrastination, lack of courage, fear of failure, etc. The world does not lack idealistic and insightful people; in fact, we have enough of them to bring the change and innovation necessary to save the world. The problem is that we have more individuals with ideas who have no intention of taking any step further beyond coming up with the concepts than we have people who are ready to act. They can visualize the success and even help create the opportunity for other people who cannot even conceive the most straightforward ideas but are willing to seize every opportunity that life throws at them. These individuals can sit down at a place and tell you how to do everything. You can see that their vision is real, and their ideas are unparalleled, yet you wonder why they cannot merely act on it. They are just suffering from what I will call the action deficiency syndrome. The reason I am taking the time to explain this is to help you recognize this dream-killer syndrome and to suggest ways to deal with it. There are so many pathological conditions floating around, and the last thing you want to do is to add one unofficial syndrome to your problem list.

The initial step in combating action deficiency syndrome is first to recognize that you are exhibiting the symptoms. If you notice that you have so many great ideas yet have never acted on any of your thoughts or visions, then pick one (the simplest, actionable) of all your numerous ideas and work on it. Make it a part of your schedule for the next six months and watch out for the results. Considering that this could be the first time you are handling a project or acting on your idea, you should not expect 100% success. You need to give room for failure to avoid crashing when the result is not favorable. If peradventure, you don't get an advantageous outcome, go through your process step by step and make a list of the failure points to figure out if there was anything you could have done better or differently within each step of the process. Ask questions and learn from people who have accomplished similar goals and apply the lessons learned next time. It is essential not to replicate your failures.

On the other hand, if you have deployed the right strategies necessary to make your lifelong dream a reality, then you must be careful about "dream-killers." These are individuals that are almost always pessimistic about every and anything. They see failure where others see success. They will give you nearly a million reasons why they think your dream will never become a success story. If you are not careful, they will cause you to doubt even the things you are most sure about yourself. I believe that so many things are possible. However, the ability to toll this path and carry the people around you along the same line of optimism requires exceptional skill. It is about time to view the word 'impossible' as a personal challenge. Sometimes realities need to be bent to unfold the things that we do not know yet, but which are possible. Therefore, it is okay to share your dreams with others, but you should be careful to recognize dream-killer traits. Remember that it is your dream, and you do not need the world's permission to execute it. The ability to dream is available to everyone, yes, but it requires planning and the subsequent actions that one must take to make the dream a reality.

Finally, reward yourself from time to time and celebrate the everyday little wins that bring you closer and closer to your dreams' actualization. Seek help from the right source when necessary, and do not die in silence. Sometimes people get into a tight corner where everything becomes almost unbearable, and all they can think about is to quit. Nonetheless, when you think back and review the history behind other people's success stories, you will realize that most of them were not quitters. So, hang in there, follow these strategies, and see how you can make your dream come true. It is a brand-new day, and each day is the first day of the rest of your life. Make your dream a reality. If you cannot make all your dreams come true, at least, start with one today, give it your best, and believe in your strength.

Chapter 3

Love the Person in the Mirror

Chapter Highlight
Your most indispensable asset is YOU! Love YOU, value YOU, believe in YOU, challenge YOU, and encourage YOU. Whatever you do, don't liquidate YOU!

It is hard to forget an encounter I had with a young lady back in my college days. I was studying in the mini Pharmacy college library (or better still, a reading room as we called it because it didn't have much of a library to it). A few minutes later, another student came in and joined me at the same table. I focused on the subject matter I was trying to understand and would have preferred not to be distracted, but I lifted my head and said hi to her and continued studying. Then she said, "you are so beautiful, Precious." Without focusing so much on the compliment expressed in that sentence due to the pressure of the moment, I lifted my head again, looked at her, smiled, and said, "thank you" as courtesy demands (thinking that we can now concentrate on studying since we are in the reading room). Then she went on and on about how she is the ugliest person in her class and the entire school (thank goodness she did not say the world as a whole, at least I have something to work with). First, I was sitting down there, wondering why we are talking about being beautiful and ugly in the heat of the moment when we have final exams all week. However, I realized she was serious when she continued to lament how she is very short, with ugly eyes, nose, fingers, legs, etc. She basically described every part of her body as very ugly, with specific details. I have heard so many people say one or two things they don't like about their looks, but never have I heard anyone hate every single part of their body as I have just heard. I have occasionally lamented over my kinky hair. Still, I finally embraced the texture as I realized that the silky straight hairs could not hold braids together as I watch the twists and knots unravel almost immediately. Thereafter, I overlooked my complaints and counted my blessings.

However, this is not the occasional frizzy hair issue or claiming to be 5 feet 8 inches tall when you are 5 feet and 5 inches tall, as a few ladies would confess. This girl did not like a single thing about herself. She was very soft-spoken, with a peaceful tone, and for a minute, I could not associate her gentle nature with the expressions that just came out of her mouth. I still hear that voice in my head, and I sincerely admire her intonation, as it comes with so much calmness. Honestly, I was not in the mood to counsel anyone at that moment due to academic pressure, but I had to pause and take a long but focused look at her, from head to toe, while trying to figure out what to say to her. She was initially confused about my gaze but suddenly started laughing and wondered what I was looking at as I continued the long stare, running my eyes from her head to her toes a few times.

Chapter Highlight

Instead of blemishes, start to look for your unique endowments and you will smile more often.

I was taken aback by her unfriendly description of herself. I have never heard anyone describe herself as she did. In her eyes, she sees the ugliest young woman not just among the students in her class, but in the entire university. I was silent for several minutes as I continued to look at her. I was astonished as I did not see the person she had just described (except for being petite, though), but she is by far not the shortest person I have seen. I was even more lost for words because I feared she might not believe what I was going to say. Knowing that I am not a psychologist or a professional counselor, and this one is far beyond my natural gift of motivation and inspiration, I had to ask God quietly to help me, so I can help this young woman to see the beauty in her. So, I looked at her once again and said, "I have been wondering whom you have been describing because that person is not the one in front of me right now."

Then I said, for a start, you have the best hair texture I have seen around here. I enquired; how much do you spend to keep your hair this good? She asked, "what do you mean?" Then I responded, "Well, I take that to mean you spend little to no money? She said, "yes." I smiled and said, "that is a big blessing, my dear." Then I added, by the way, your eyebrow is beautiful; you probably need to thread it sometimes so that it can be well aligned. She smiled and asked, are you for real? I said, never been more sincere. I picked up a few more things I admired about her and highlighted the uniqueness and the beauty. For instance, I told her that if my voice were as calm as hers, nobody would ever be angry with anything I say, no matter how critical the underlying message may be. Then, I added, by the way, you can ask around if you don't know me that well; I am not known to flatter, I say it as I see it. She immediately became enlivened, and we talked about other things and became good acquaintances after that day. I could not see her for too long after that day as she was in a different program and may have transferred or changed majors.

I share this story because I know that this young lady is not alone in this self-hate struggle. In her case, it is a matter of her physical appearance, whereas, for some people, it could be the lack of self-confidence that translates to significantly low self-esteem. Instead of blemishes, start to look for your unique endowments, and you will smile more often. For instance, her voice is a unique asset in the meditation and sleep hypnosis industry.

I occasionally watch children's program on television because they are not only decent, but quite imaginative and educative, and most importantly, because I currently have a toddler who makes sure our television is perpetually playing these programs. Therefore, I cannot help but enjoy these programs since they are almost always on. On one of the programs, the ant was playing basketball with other animals, (which in my opinion is an overly ambitious sport for an ant), but it was a struggle throughout. The ant became quite angry and wished to become a giant, which was possible in their little imaginative world. However, when he finally became a giant, it was so inconvenient to burrow in the soil or play hide and seek, and he eventually accepted the uniqueness of being an ant.

Now, before you crucify me for daring to insult your intelligence with an example from a mere toddler's TV program, permit me to say that this experience is an endless struggle in the real adult world. There is this incessant expression of dissatisfaction that comes from a place of ingratitude for what we already have, because we are focused on what we do not have. We always concentrate more on what we don't have that others have, rather than exploring our unique attributes, which the world needs. It is different if others are putting you down; at least then, you can probably pick yourself up. It is worst when you put yourself down because there is almost no hope of rising. The worst battle to fight is the battle you fight with yourself because nobody even knows such war is going on, so it could go on for far too long.

In order to be in the place of love, you have to take charge of what goes on in your mind and conquer the most significant battlefield of all times - the mind. Conquering this battle starts by first recognizing that this battle exists and the impact it has on your life. The next step is to accept the things about you that you cannot change, mainly your physical appearance. Remember that this chapter of your life was already written by your creator and written with a purpose in mind. So, don't waste the energy intended for other phases of your life in self-dislike. Don't get me wrong, you can enhance yourself to an extent naturally possible, but you really must accept who you are from a place of love. A heart full of hate for itself is not capable of giving wholehearted love to another. Self-hate can also be due to the feeling of incapability and unacceptance, which creates a unique hollow. These hollows are dangerous because if not appropriately filled with gratitude and love, it becomes a blank canvas for others to load up based on their definition of who they think you are. In which case, you are most likely to buy into their reports and begin to see incapability where capability once thrived.

Happiness is a choice, and so is love. You can control what affects you by making a conscious effort to avoid undue comparisons of yourself to other people. You can emulate good things that you admire from other people as a growth strategy. On the other hand, comparing yourself to other people often results in self-hate, and this is quite unfair to YOU as a person because no two individuals are the same. While we may look alike on the outside, our circumstances and situations make us different. Hence you are comparing oranges to grapefruits here. True beauty comes from within, and when the heart is full of love and appreciation, the external features cannot help but radiate the inner expressions on the outside. That is why people glow when they find love, irrespective of their physical characteristics.

Chapter Highlight
Resist the urge to compare yourself to others. You are neither worse nor better. You are your yardstick; just be a better YOU!!!

Again, remember, love comes from the inside. You cannot give what you don't have. If you don't know love, you won't recognize it when you see it. You should not measure your love for yourself by the number of people who love and appreciate you. There are cases when people live in self-guilt because they can never understand why a particular person hates them so much and never see any good in them. It is easy to think that you may have done something wrong or even erroneously believe that you are not worthy of their love. It is hard to believe it, but the truth is that their hate towards you may not have anything to do with anything you have done wrong. There are so many reasons why some people cannot show love, so you cannot quit loving yourself because one or two people failed to love you irrespective of their position in your life. Your life is counting on your love, and it will be such a disappointment for your love for you not to count when it matters most. If you want love, start with the person you see in the mirror.

Chapter Highlight
Remember, love comes from the inside. You cannot give what you don't have. If you don't know love, you won't recognize it when you see it. If you want love, start with the person you see in the mirror.

Finally, scan yourself outwardly and inwardly from head to toe and make a mental note of all the things that need acknowledgment from a place of gratitude. Part of this mental note is to learn who you are and your unique areas of strength. Compare these unique attributes to the things you don't like about yourself, and you will be amazed at what you will discover. You will find that you have more to appreciate than you know. When you learn and appreciate what you are good at, you will recognize that you do not need validation from anyone; that is when self-confidence and self-esteem come into play

Chapter 4

The Influences that Make us:
Our Root and the Uncommon Sources

Chapter Highlight
Successful people are in constant motion, and they are both physically and cognitively alert. They are inventively disruptive, undoubtedly motivated, and passionately insightful. They are not necessarily highly educated or technologically savvy. Instead, the common denominator is passion translated to action.

It is natural and hence expected that people may want to blame their historical roots or family background when life is not as favorable as expected. Such individuals will rather spend years blaming their parents, uncles, friends, failed government, etc., for their existing mishaps and failures. I am not ignorant of the negative consequences of an unfavorable socioeconomic background or failed government; however, as I alluded to in the initial chapter of this book, those are the uncontrollable chapter(s) of your life. It is almost unhealthy to continue to blame history year after year without making reasonable efforts to turn things around. Whether history handed you sweet tangerines or sour lemons, it is up to you to redirect and spearhead subsequent chapters of your life. You cannot blame your past forever. At some point, you will have to concentrate on the present so that you can create your best history; one you will be happy with the story someday. A good leader takes ownership of the results of his/her actions and takes accountability for negative consequences while exploring ways to achieve a better outcome. A courageous Life CEO sees unique opportunity where others see failure.

    As I think about my life's journey and the influences that have inspired my growth and contributed to some, if not most, of my success stories, I cannot help but revisit my root as my number one source of influence. There is a constant recall of my upbringing, the supportive foundation, and the love. The memory also identifies some of the struggles and the hope against odds created by a failed government and unfriendly economy. It also includes the faith and belief in a brighter and better tomorrow that will eventually cause a family to uproot and transplant an entire household to a strange land outside the comfort of an already established financial security and the support system provided by extended family and relatives. I remember the community lifestyle that engenders the zeal to succeed and be a helping hand to others. The understanding that a child is not raised by his/her parents alone, but by the entire community. The latter means that your grade teacher or another parent/adult has the right and responsibility to discipline you if found misbehaving, and it will not be considered abuse.

 I am one of the many that would come to America as an adult who is already married with children. I have listened to some other people's stories, including stories from the early immigrants' descendants who now consider America their own. I have also heard stories of anguish, distress, violence, abuse, and subsequent mental instability. However, I have heard enough to suggest that our root, when visited with gratitude, builds a more robust and better future, even if it is for the most insignificant things.

 I often imagine the number of flights that land each day with yet another individual who would be coming to the United States of America for the first time. From Africa alone, several flights, KLM, Lufthansa, Virgin Atlantic (for a while), British Airways, United Airlines, Qatar Airlines, Delta Air, Ethiopian Airline, to mention but a few, depart every day and headed to a chosen dreamland. I am not referring to the tourists and visitors who come periodically to have some good time and head back home in a matter of weeks. The latter has neither the need nor the intention to spend more than four weeks outside the shores of Africa. In this case, I am referring to the individuals who are relocating in pursuit of a dream.

In some cases, the plan has been analyzed and well comprehended. For some others, the dream is either beclouded with confusion and disarray or never conceived. Some may occasionally ask, "why am I here?" For the latter, it is evident that life was deluxe; no tears or struggles, no stress or distress, no strife or pain, just rosy, plentiful, and golden. How smooth and sweet! The only reason you left the comfort of your home country is to put the icing on the cake and some garnishing on an already rich cocktail. There was no wait time for your student visa, or better still, your investment visa (a process that grants resident permits to wealthy investors). The airplane ticket was not a problem either, and the established USA or European bank account was already waiting. There is no need to pay house rent or mortgage because your parents already paid for a house in your name. Have I just painted a picture of you? There is nothing wrong with the image represented above. In case you have not figured it out yet, this describes the lives of several young men and women who are sent out of the shores of most underdeveloped countries by their parents to get western education for the furtherance of a vast family empire at home. The main question, though, is, will you be able to keep up with the expectations at the home front and provide the same level of comfort to your successors, or will you break the records (literally) and initiate a cycle of poverty for your generations to come?

For some others, life was not that rosy but not miserable either. Visa was not that easy to come by since you do not have high and mighty connections. The embassy may have pushed back your interview date a few times to accommodate the first-class citizens (the former set of people described above), but that's the least of your worry. All you want is a visa to your dreamland! Air tickets may not have been easy to pay for either, but who cares? You finally made it out to the western world, and that's what matters. Your dream clock has just started ticking, and a more comfortable lifestyle for your family at home becomes not only your burden but your motivator. All you can think about is how to make them even more comfortable.

Please permit me to introduce the very brilliant young folks; magnificent, superb, bright, and vivid, yet, quite pitiful, miserable, and undeniably wretched, whose most significant assets are not available to the highest bidder on the bestselling stock market. Their brain is on fire, their brilliance is unparalleled, and nothing can stop it, not even the constant threat of hunger. Instead, deprivation to them becomes a driving force for success. The only possible reason they can see the four walls of a western university building is because of their outstanding academic performance that strikes the loudest chords across many nations. Thank goodness for the fair distribution of gifts and talents. The admission letter comes, and tuition is covered because it was part of the scholarship award! Finally, there is a reason to smile in their family; father and mother are happy, excited, and proud of their brilliant child. It dawns on everyone at the break of day; tears start rolling, sleep becomes a luxury, nights become longer, everyone pacing up and down and gazing at the ceiling and looking for nonexistent answers. Then it finally clicks!!! Ten plots of land, fifteen acres of pineapple orchard, twenty farmlands, all sold in one day, at a giveaway price, to purchase a plane ticket and cover other expenses outside of tuition. What a sacrifice! It is a sacrifice made for a son or a daughter without thinking twice, a selfless sacrifice made without minding how and when the next meal will come. The self-depriving gift from an African father and mother! The sacrifice that hopefully influences success and rewrites destinies for several generations to come.

I am not sure who you are or if you have tried to imagine playing any of the roles illustrated above and how much it would have influenced you. I may have painted the African root image because that is the root I know, but it is just a simple platform meant to enliven something in you geared towards success. Interestingly enough, the story is similar in some way, irrespective of your nationality. We hear these stories every day, even in America. A brilliant, hardworking son or daughter from a low socioeconomic background gets an acceptance letter into a prestigious university due to academic excellence. The family forgets for a minute amidst their rejoicing that there is no money for housing fees and feeding. Then suddenly, like a spark, it finally clicks, and the momentary joy turns to sorrow when someone suddenly asks, "wait, how do we pay for this?" The mom says, "I will pick up a second job, and the dad says; I will work overtime to support." The sacrifice is universal.

Regardless of your country of origin (western world or third world), we all have a root, and we have stories, short, long, exciting, depressing, good or bad, be it as it may, however, today and the future is in your hands. Whatever the case may be, let your root be a source of courage and not fear, spark the light of ambition, and quench the urge to blame. If your life is currently miserable, I hope that the misery becomes the force that propels the discipline needed to sustain your ambition and the desire to succeed and not just survive.

Every time I go down the memory lane and childhood experiences, I cannot help but remember every moment I spent with my siblings and other extended relatives who shared our space with us at any given time. I remember a young girl (probably nineteen or twenty years old) who came to live with us because the mother wanted her in our house since my mom was a better disciplinarian and would help the young girl be a better person. I was sixteen at the time. There I was, with my sister, feeling bad that we were never allowed to go out freely like other girls, and here comes another mother, wishing that her daughter stayed indoors like us. Of course, she did not last in our house. She left one day after asking me how we survive with the 24-hour curfew as young girls. At this time, I was already used to it, and it did not bother me anymore. I started wondering what people would be looking for outside, or better still, why a girl would be out at night and in a nightclub.

Being indoors enhanced my creativity and critical thinking skills, and I used the opportunity to pick up on some domestic skills.

Chapter Highlight
Success wants an active learner who is open-minded and willing to learn from anybody.

I picked up quite a few things from these extended siblings. In some cases, I learned what not to do, and in other times I recognized something that I ought to start doing. I gathered one or two things about praying from one of them (a much older lady) who lived with us to help in my mom's business. She had a ritual of kneeling by the bed to pray every night in preparation for bedtime. Daily prayer was not a routine in my family at the time. When she saw my interest, she made me join her every night. I was probably ten years old at that time. This lady will fall asleep multiple times while praying, and I will tap her on the shoulder and call her name when I don't hear any other words from her after a few minutes. I wondered why she wouldn't just go to bed and give up praying for only one night if she was that sleepy. Or possibly make the prayer shorter. It eventually occurred to me that this is something she believed strongly in and was thus showing dedication.

Since my family was not so much into praying at that time, I was grateful to have someone to pray with, even if she fell asleep so many times and muttered things I could not even understand because she was sleeping and praying at the same time.

In the case of the young girl that came to live with us so she can be better disciplined, I learned a lot from that experience, even though she found it unpleasant to be indoors and monitored at all times. Now, when I look back, I appreciate the home that raised me. Though it was far from being a lot of fun, someone else considered our grass greener in the area of discipline and wanted her daughter to be a part of it.

I remember following my maternal grandmother (who is now late) to the market (a small flea market) located in a tiny city in Imo State, Nigeria, one calm evening. I should be about 12 years old at this time, and I still have the image of a young woman in probably her early twenties, who, by her language and a slight sense I could make from what she was saying, was from a neighboring African country. A public transport minibus had just dropped her off not too long ago. She was young and beautiful, appeared very harmless but with recognizable mental issues. She had on a clean set of clothes that will eventually turn to rags as she lives in the market square for months that turn into years (as is customary with individuals in such a mental state in my country). She was singing a gospel song ("I love that man of Galilee") that caught my attention as I withdrew my hand from my grandmother's grip and stood still to listen to her. I wanted to learn the song and register the lyrics, so I paid close attention. Till today, each time I sing that song, I cannot help but cast my mind back to that encounter as I pondered how much devotion, love, and reverence she gave to her Lord and God even in her mental state. She taught me something about faith and gratitude.

Once again, it was Christmas time many years later, and my parents took us out shopping. The market was bustling, the sun was crushing hot, the humidity was unbearable, vehicle horns are going off and on, and people are nothing close to friendly. Just so we are clear, this is not the kind of shopping mall some of you are probably familiar with, or any decent department store. I am referring to the type of shopping environment where your car is parked close to two miles away from the stores, and you are struggling to make sure you buy everything on your list before all the stores close at 5 PM!

As we maneuvered through the endless crowd, I saw a young man, crippled and seated on the floor under the heat of the sun and singing with all his strength while sweating profusely as if his life was dependent on the song. In his musical piece (which was in my native language), he expressed so much gratitude to God. I stood still, almost pinned to the ground as I looked at him in utter bewilderment and wondered why he was so grateful considering his situation. He did not even have any collection basket like other beggars. He never cared if people dropped money or not. His eyes were closed half the time as he sang so passionately and gratefully. Then again, as I thought more about it, I realized what he was grateful for; it was for life! Though he appeared helpless and hopeless, he displayed so much strength and courage. He was living above hope and expressing the joy that even the affluent lacked. He helped me to appreciate my own life even more.

What is my point? We sure do have a lot to learn from the people around us as well as our environment. The influences that make us don't always come from the expected places. They don't always come from the most experienced individuals, the aged, the intelligent, or the brilliant. They come from everyone and everywhere.

Chapter Highlight

You may ask, what is there to learn from the supposed foolish person? What is there to learn from a mediocre? The real question is, what is there not to learn?

I am the kind of individual that learns from every and anybody. I read and learn from many people, people with both success stories and people with everyday failures but still refused to fail. Success wants an active learner who is open-minded and willing to learn from anybody.

I am open to learning from the old and the young. I listen to the rich and the poor, the experienced and the supposedly inexperienced, and learn from both the wise and the foolish. I study people who have dared to do something different and learn from those who have continued to do the same thing despite unfavorable outcomes. I am often impressed by people who have surpassed unimaginable barriers and limitations. People who have disrupted mediocrity's pleasant comfort and stepped up and out to break fresh grounds have thus occupied the kingly seats.

You may have heard that there are two kinds of stories: those that have happy endings and those that do not end too well. Everyone has a story, and life itself is a story. Some learn from their own stories, while others learn from other people's stories. I choose to learn from both. I learn from big dreamers and people who are highly optimistic and yet observe the pessimistic. I am sure you must have gotten my point by now; our environment and the people around us provide us with endless learning opportunities!

One thing remains apparent; there are two categories of people, the successful and the unsuccessful. Successful people are in constant motion, and they are both physically and cognitively alert. They are inventively disruptive, undoubtedly motivated, and passionately insightful. They are not necessarily highly educated or technologically savvy. Instead, the common denominator is passion translated to action. You may ask, what is there to learn from the supposed foolish person? What is there to learn from a mediocre? The real question is, what is there not to learn? Have you not heard that the foolish confirms the wisdom of the wise? I firmly believe that the unfavorable outcomes of the mediocre encourage exceptional and extraordinary talents.

A good story is not just one with a happy ending because people like me find both good and bad stories resourceful. If every story we tell ends well, there would not be much room for improvement. If every business we venture into turns out to be pleasantly successful as anticipated, then there won't be the need for brainstorming activities towards problem-solving and growth. Therefore, I learn from every story. I like to know why and how people eventually end up with great success stories after a considerably sad one. How did they survive self-pity and the blame game? How were they able to start a new chapter at the end of an unfavorable one? Did they get permission from their inner self, who was possibly lost in self-pity and disappointment, to restart a new story? How did the self-reinvention happen? How were they able to unlearn the things and habits that landed them to failure in the first place? These questions and many more are what I pay attention to and strive to find their possible answers. So, I read every story, I listen, and I learn. I learn not because I am afraid to fail, but I pay attention because I don't want to become a failure. To be a failure is to be scared to fail.

The purpose of this chapter is to encourage you to be an active learner who translates both good and bad lessons to pleasant outcomes. You are encouraged to be the kind of individual that pays attention to his/her surrounding, with ears attentive to the stories that our environment tells. This kind of story is such that regular and inattentive people may not recognize even if it is a reverberating echo. That level of attentiveness is the difference between you and everybody else.

Since we also know that there are two distinct categories of people, we can make a conscious effort to make the right shift towards success by surrounding ourselves with the right people. I believe that star individuals do have certain innate traits and natural abilities. However, beyond natural endowments, the primary key to excellence and success is the possession of mental toughness engendered by determination and zeal. I have been in several high-stress situations, though I maintained an appreciable level of mental calmness. I am not sure I enjoyed those instances; neither was the experience comfortable. However, one must develop the tough skin needed for such situations. Some pressure moments help bring out the best in us, help us unleash the inner potentials that we probably never knew were there, and help us commit to self-improvement if we don't give up in the interim.

More so, fixing our eyes on the finish line make it easier to rise multiple times even though we fail a thousand times. It is somewhat unrealistic to attain our long-term goals without the small, negligible achievements we make here and there. Our commitment and mental readiness for the small wins and failures along the path to success help us attain the ultimate goal.

Look around you; the world is evolving daily. Reinvention is necessary at some point, especially in these present times, to overcome stagnation. Reinvention is a challenge for everyone who is passionately motivated to succeed. Keeping yourself motivated throughout your life is as important as achieving your most important life goals.

Reinventing ourselves sometimes requires that we constantly evaluate our performances and recognize where improvement is needed. By so doing, we can ensure that we do not reproduce our mistakes but instead develop the self-confidence needed to build on our expertise and excellence. These are the influences that make us. Your ability to recognize your sources of power and how to make appropriate use of the resources around you guarantees that you have the right words on your life's storybook and that you are leading yourself in the right direction each day. Therefore, your root and the stories (both good and bad) of the people around you should be a source of positive influence towards leading you right.

Chapter 5

The Good Outlier

Chapter Highlight
The gift of choice is the most powerful of all. Let the choices you make show that you are in control. After all, it is your life.

To effectively lead your life, you may have to be an outlier occasionally. Outliers are not always bad. In this case, I am referring to you being a good outlier. There is absolutely nothing wrong with being the only one doing it right and possibly showing others the right path to follow. It is okay to mess up the symmetrical bell curve of societal trends and expectations. Do not believe the unfounded fallacy that you have to belong to or go with the flow. People face excessive pressure in today's world now more than ever because we are trying so hard to fit into a socially acceptable description of who we should be. There are several unverified and unwarranted standards set, and society will not stop attempting to embarrass you if you decide to be the odd one out. The problem is not that these standards are unwarranted; the bigger problem is that we do not even know who is setting them. We are just following blindly without knowing where the person is headed or who we are following. As a distinctive individual, you should be in control of your life, and your standards should be based on your values, faith, and belief system.

Unfortunately, we cannot go back in time and excuse ourselves from this time and era where we are constantly under pressure to fit into a socially acceptable frame or template. However, you can exempt yourself from obliging the society's template where square pegs are forced onto triangular holes and vice versa. Therefore, to please them, you succumb to their pressure by constantly waiting for them to validate your activities, what you eat or wear. You jump on board their decisions even when it does not make much sense to you. Otherwise, tell me why somebody will wake up one day and come up with the idea of a ripped jeans design, and we so willingly embrace it. We even pay more money just because they designed and validated the concept when we should be asking for some change to make up for the holes on the fabric! Some of them are far worse than others; the rips are barely held by a single string of thread that you are almost afraid to spot clean them, let alone wash them without turning them into shreds. My son was wearing one the other day, and I couldn't help but shake my head as I asked him how much he paid for it. You can call me old school, but I am not paying full price for a ripped pair of jeans! I have nothing against innovative designers; I encourage disruptive innovation. However, this is just an example, and the point of this chapter is to awaken your sense of personal leadership. If you are leading your life, you cannot always only follow where others lead. It is okay to make a left where others make a right turn, and vice versa. As a matter of fact, it is entirely okay to make a U-turn half-way through a path that runs contrary to what you stand for. Especially when you don't know or don't understand who is leading you and the direction you are headed. If, on the other hand, you believe you are on the right path, don't change your course just because everybody else is going in the opposite direction. Your life is your personal agenda, and you are accountable for it, so leading it right is your ultimate responsibility.

Even though you are under pressure to fit into this socially acceptable frame, it is essential to know that the pressure might be a test of your inner strength and integrity after all. Though people might be antagonistic of you, they may be secretly admiring your inner strength and courage. As a result, you become a failure to yourself and to them when you fail to stand your ground. Conversely, if you are strong enough to stand your ground and stay true to your belief system, you may have some converts someday. It may not be right away, but it is a possibility.

About ten years ago, I attended an annual conference of the American Pharmacists Association (APhA) in Washington DC, alongside a few other pharmacy students from my school. There were close to 20,000 people in attendance, including pharmacists, pharmacy students, pharmacy technicians, and vendors representing either a sponsoring corporate entity or a pharmaceutical company. Part of our registration package was the New Practitioner's night out at a somewhat decent nightclub. That would be my first time in a nightclub, and I also thought that since it was a professional outing, maybe this one will be "professional." So, I went with my classmates. I was in my early thirties, but there I was, assuming that this night club will be different and that it was okay because everyone was going, plus the fact that a professional organization arranged it. How dumb of me! A nightclub is a nightclub, and there is nothing professional about it. So, we walked in, and people were just too close for comfort, everyone had a glass of wine/liquor in their hands, and some were already tipsy even though the night was barely starting. Smells of cigarettes filled the room. You would almost think there is a valet guy outside and everyone has to drop off keys with him, except this time, this valet guy is invisible, and people are not dropping off car keys, but the keys to their sense of reasoning checked out on the door as they walked in.

    I could not breathe; I was literally suffocating. I searched within myself and wondered what I was doing in this environment. I was uncomfortable and instantly unhappy, yet most people (if not all) seemed happy, were dancing, and into the moment. It was as though people just wanted to forget who they are for a moment and have fun, no matter the outcome. For me, this seems like a very costly fun from a health and moral perspective. We had just walked in less than 3 minutes, so we were still all together in our little group. I looked at one of the girls from my school straight in the face and sternly too. I did not utter a word, but she knew what was on my mind, and she started laughing. My look was more like, "What are we doing here, or better still, what am I doing here?" She beckoned on the other classmates and said, "let's go back outside and put this woman in a taxi so she can go back to the hotel." That was how I went back to my hotel room and had my good night's rest.

How I left the club became one of our "after conference" stories as they would not stop joking about it and telling this story to those that were not in attendance. By the way, I appreciate that my colleagues went out of their way to make sure I was safe. It is always lovely to be with a team of friends who have your interest at heart and who will respect your values and standards. I appreciate the spirit of camaraderie. After all, no one forced me to be there. I made flawed assumptions and followed the crowd, but I was not ashamed to be the only outlier in her thirties who has never been to a nightclub. Still no regrets and no shame about leaving the place where I know I do not belong.

Chapter Highlight
Don't let the opinion of a few people hinder your success that could potentially be of interest to the larger public.

Sometimes people follow the crowd because it represents the majority, and it is easy to blindly assume that the group ought to know what they are doing or where they are going. It could also be because you don't want to be ridiculed or called names, so you give up your leadership role and play a follower in matters that concern your own life. It is okay to be a follower when it comes to other things but not with decisions that could negatively affect your life. You should have no apologies because it is your life. If your friends cannot respect you and your choices that stem from good morals and personal judgment, then they are not qualified to be called friends in the first place.

Being unnecessarily apologetic and the constant struggle to please friends is one of the primary reasons why many young adults make mistakes that sometimes affect and jeopardize the rest of their lives. Meanwhile, those who pressured them into such mistakes move around with no regrets. The problem is the fear of being ridiculed in front of others. It is your life; if it doesn't feel right, don't think twice about saying no. You are ultimately responsible for leading yourself in the right direction. When people present choices in a manner that puts you in an instant position to make an impulsive decision, it is okay to travel the path with less traffic which may seem unpopular at the time. The key to taking the right approach is to recognize the signs of unwarranted pressure to succumb to peers' influence. At that point, you know there is a need for you to immediately activate and apply common sense and good judgment over irrational suggestions and inclinations.

The health care sector, for instance, focuses on research and evidence-based practice. In this setting, facts and figures are necessary to back up each clinical decision. The result of the latter is a uniform approach to care. I have seen situations where patients are convinced about all options available to them before (if it ever happens), listening to what they have to say about themselves. Whereas, listening first to understand their unique characteristics and history could inform, if not sway, the therapeutic decision. The health care environment is one arena where intuition is not the order of the day. When a patient comes in and says, "I have used this before, and I know it works for me" or "I have been through this before, and this was what happened before the incident," etc., what often happens? We look for documented evidence in our medical history book, and in the absence of such, advice otherwise. I am not in any way undermining the importance and significance of evidence-based medicine, but to recognize that the absence of documented proof does not always mean a lack of evidence.

We are always trying to know what everyone else is doing. Why do we have to reinvent what other people are doing? Especially when the recorded outcome is unfavorable or when there is no proven comparison against alternatives? The national standard becomes our yardstick and customary practice, irrespective of the societal flaws that may negatively sway these numbers. Most integrated corporate systems are constantly following and copying methods from their associate facilities or entities. When someone presents a novel idea, one of the first questions becomes, who else does this within the corporation?

Meanwhile, there are lessons to be learned if we can expand our imagination beyond the confines of people who look like us, think like us, and whose results mirror ours. Who says you cannot rise and teach others to copy? My advice to you is, don't let the opinion of a few people or the generic prescription of a narrow-minded crowd hinder your success that could potentially be of benefit to the larger public.

Sometimes there is just nothing out there, and that is when intuition and innovation come in handy. You are allowed to take that leap of faith sometimes as the CEO of your life, even if no one has threaded that path previously. Greater reliance on market research and public opinion has cost us our inner and accumulated wisdom. We ought to recognize that sometimes there is nothing on the history page to read; there may not be any directions to follow, apart from the moral upbringings and personal convictions that stem from more profound beliefs. Sometimes, our reliance and dependence on what everybody else is doing and applying a uniform process have beclouded our innovative and creative minds, whereby we conduct experiments with the result in mind. Being a regular follower affects your ability to anticipate and explore both scientific and nonscientific surprises.

Who says you are not allowed to do something that no one else is doing or has done? Who says you cannot create your custom? Who says you cannot change a practice you do not like? Who says you must conform to the celebrated but irrational and unreasonable norm?

I once had a student who got inspired to dress up a little more nicely, especially when giving presentations after being on my experiential rotation for six weeks. While with a different preceptor, she gave a presentation and was in semi-business attire. Everyone in the room, including other preceptors, wondered why she looked like she was heading to a board room for an interview. She quickly shared her source of inspiration and how it has changed her mindset. A colleague of mine who witnessed the discussion told me that this student said, "Precious inspired me each day while I was on her rotation to appear my best." While this colleague was sharing this with me, she mentioned that she used to dress up nicely to work until a physician told her that someone cannot be intelligent and look good at the same time. In other words, smartness and looking good are inversely related, according to this physician. As untrue as it is, that statement caused this colleague to consider a dress-down approach so that she can be regarded as being competent. It also reminded me of what another colleague said during my residency training, "nobody has time here to look good." Being well-dressed to this individual means you are not working hard enough. So, here we are, having more and more people buy into this ideology when it is evident that there is no relationship between outward appearance and brilliance. Somebody's belief is almost becoming most people's ideology. If anything, I consider the reverse to be the case; intelligence should be synonymous with good looking. Therefore, I choose to stand by the truth that I know, and it does not matter if I stand alone.

There are also other instances where people begin to doubt themselves because of peer pressure. Interestingly enough, when we mention peer pressure, we automatically think about the most vulnerable population (kids and teenagers) and hence fail to recognize the unpopular victims (adults). Frankly, adults are under constant pressure from peers but hardly recognize it. Some of it can be positive, of course (like being at the gym and seeing so many fit individuals with good abs while you are struggling to lose 1 or 2 pounds). It would be better if we are only worried about the positive peer pressures. The truth is that we are in a constant struggle to please friends, colleagues, and people in the same social organization or group. The unfortunate thing is that we don't even realize we are under such pressure.

Recognizing the presence of such pressure is key to making the right move to overcome it. It helps you to know the best way to react by recognizing when you are succumbing versus standing by your will and decision. When I think about the day-to-day peer pressure that we often don't acknowledge, one or two examples come to mind. A few years back, when I was completing my postdoctoral residency program, all the residents would usually meet Wednesday afternoons (for approximately 4hrs) for a weekly training conference. The meeting was a way for us to interact with residents from other facilities within the organization. There were probably fifteen of us, and I was the only one with three little kids waiting for me at home as well as in a concurrent master's degree program. One other resident had kids too, but the kids were with her husband at their home state. At the end of the conference, the residents would want us to go out and socialize, which was a good thing, but it was not convenient for me, so I found myself saying "no" to them several times. I said "no" too many times that it became apparent that I was such an outlier. Sometimes I could see the expression of disappointment on some faces. Other times, it felt as though I was not a team player or one who did not like to socialize. Of course, I explained why I could not go, though I am not sure my explanation seemed reasonable enough to them. They probably did not realize they were putting me under pressure with their requests, making things more difficult in such situations. However, I had to stand my ground and stick to my decision for two reasons:

1. I had promised myself that I would find the right balance between the program I am doing (which is quite demanding of my time) and taking care of my children in the best way possible by being there for them whenever I can.
2. Most of the suggested events for the socialization were things I don't enjoy doing.

I asked myself these questions as I drove home one evening after declining the invitation yet again:

A. Why should I go out to socialize just because others want me to, after being out for so long already when I have three little kids waiting for me at home?

B. Why does it matter what they say or think if I know, I am doing the right thing?

In dealing with peer pressure, you need to remember and consider your circumstances and preferences. You should always be at the center of the decision and not the other way around. If there is any time that you are permitted to be selfish, it is when faced with such pressure. It helps you to think clearly in the heat of the moment.

 I will share another more recent scenario, mainly because it was less apparent in the beginning that the pressure was on. While working at a previous institution, you are likely to be greeted by someone on a golf cart once you park your car. Usually, they will give you a ride to the closest entrance to help reduce your walking time. As much as I appreciate this service and have also used it many times, particularly during the summer, there came a time when I decided to walk more, so I did not want to use the ride anymore. After I decided to pick up on the steps, this particular person would come to give me a lift each morning. This individual was so timely that it was as if he knows when I leave my house and calculates my arrival accurately. He asked me if I needed a ride every morning for five consecutive days, and I said no five times. One afternoon the same week, I met someone in the elevator, whom I greeted as courtesy demands. I did not realize he was the same person because he had a different uniform, but he recognized me. Then he smiled and said jokingly, "I am the person you keep rejecting each morning when I offer to help you with a ride." It was funny that he said that, but I was more surprised that it bothered him, even though it seemed he was teasing me, so I felt terrible. I laughed and quickly apologized and explained to him that I want to walk more. What is baffling about this is how bad it makes one feel even when you are doing the right thing. Several examples of these scenarios play out each day where people will try to make you feel bad for saying no.

In some cases, you hear things like, "Why won't you go out to drink with me if truly we are friends or if you have forgiven me?" Even though the person asking you knows you don't drink. Or, "if we are cool as you claim, you should come to hang out with my friends and me." In this instance, you probably don't appreciate the company of their friends, and you may have already made it apparent. It is even more shocking that such trivial matters that would ordinarily mean nothing suddenly sends guilt vibes down your spine, and hopefully, you don't succumb to the emotional trick.

Unfortunately, we are faced with so many similar situations each day, and if we are not careful, we relinquish our will and let others lead the way. We gradually but eventually give others our steering wheel without realizing it. I hope you will pause for a moment at this point and ask yourself how many times you have handed others the steering wheel of your life. Your response will help you determine whether you have been the one leading "YOU" for the most part.

In case you were wondering how the golf cart story ended, it did not end for a while. The following day after the elevator conversation, he tried again and said, "don't tell me you will reject me again today?" I almost gave in at this point, but as always, I smiled and said, "thank you for the offer, but I am okay walking." It is not anything personal, I am sure he just wanted to show that he was providing the best service, and I sincerely appreciate it.

When faced with pressure, you should pause and decide whether it is worth giving up your steering wheel. If it is not worth it, then don't feel bad about your decision, no matter how the person makes you feel. If you are not doing anything wrong, I see no reason to go against your personal decision to satisfy someone else's desires. One rule of thumb is that if you are on the right path and can morally justify your decision, then majority opinion, whatever it is, does not count. Your ability to stand by what you know is right and proper, despite the mouth-savoring temptation to join the famous team, is what distinguishes a tremendous personal CEO from an average life manager.

    I will share something that happened to me a few times both in High school and college, which I am almost sure you may have also experienced. Do you remember being in class and the teacher asks a question, and you are sure you know the answer? Then the teacher says, if you think the answer is "A," raise your hand. You were not going to raise your hand because you are sure the answer is "B." Gradually, all the students started raising their hands one after another. Suddenly you find your hand going up because you just looked up and realized that everybody's hand was up except yours. Then the teacher smiles and says, the answer is actually "B," and you had to beat yourself up for failing to stand by your response that you were so sure was accurate. I can remember beating myself a few times for not maintaining my stand. As long as you are capable and cognitively alert, never live a life mainly guided by majority opinion where others control your life decisions. A life where your honest opinion does not count. Before you realize it, you would have become the blank sheet of paper saying, "write on me," as described in chapter one.

    Furthermore, NEVER allow wrong to magically become right just for the mere reason of majority inclination. The world wants us to follow all the time, but as a distinct individual, you alone have the ultimate responsibility to lead YOU and to lead YOU right. Only you understand your life struggles and the reason for certain decisions you have to make. Don't be sorry to walk on your unique path, don't apologize for taking the lead over your own life!

Chapter 6

Push the Limits

Chapter Highlight
Courage wants you to look past your limitations and overturn discouragements.

Limits are synonymous with restrictions, boundaries, the need to seek permission, and impossibility. The dictionary definition of limits includes "the quality or state of being limited." Understanding what the limits are, and recognizing when they occur, is the first step to finding the breaking strategy. Failure, especially repetitive ones, often brings about frustrations, and hopefully, the frustrations help bring out the best in you. When a good leader fails, the expectation is that he or she goes back to the drawing board to trace the missteps. Unfortunately, we mistakenly consider roadblocks to be limitations and often end the journey to success prematurely. Every failure or roadblock should trigger us to unleash the inner potentials that we probably never knew were there, just like the body's immune system is activated to trigger an immune response when an infection occurs. I have learned more from failures than I will ever learn from my numerous successes. It does not mean that I want to fail more or that I enjoy having unfavorable outcomes; it just means that I make every failure count by learning the hard lessons it brings with it.

Limitations should challenge our strengths; hence resistance must be applied when we face such hurdles. It is also essential to recognize that not all roadblocks, restrictions, and boundaries are limitations. Understanding the difference and pushing forward when faced with potential physical, environmental, or mental restrictions is key to breaking the limits.

I have been privileged to sit under the same roof with some of America's influential leaders and sports legends. These leaders are invited year after year as keynote speakers at a professional conference, including Bill Clinton, Collin Powell, Michelle Obama, Magic Johnson, and Condoleezza

Rice. As a personal life CEO who is open to learning something new each moment, especially about leadership strategies, I go to these opening speeches with my ears and mind unlocked to learn something new. At the most recent conference, the former US Secretary of States, Condoleezza Rice, said something that registered with me. She said, "when you see a barrier, you can do one of three things: leap over it, go around it, or go through it, but don't stand there and look at it." In my opinion, the everyday failures and obstacles we face are comparable to these barriers. You have to devise the means to either remove the obstruction or leap over it. Removing impediments requires inner strength, drive, and relentless commitment. When any of this is lacking, it becomes easy to accept and magnify the limitation without putting up any fight. There is a saying that people will always throw stones on your path, and what you make of these stones (a wall or a bridge) is your choice. Certain limitations represent the traffic stop signs, red lights, and detours we face each day. All of which requires that we take a mental stop, assess the path we are moving on, and determine whether we ought to continue straight, turn left or right, or follow an alternate route, as long as we get to our final destination.

  Some years ago, at the beginning of my pharmacy career, I searched for a job, and it was not forthcoming. I was disappointed, especially because I had put in several years of education (completed my Doctor of Pharmacy degree with an additional two-year post-doctoral pharmacy practice and Health administration residency training in a reputable healthcare organization, including a concurrent master's degree). I was even more frustrated when one of the recruiters told me that I was overqualified for the staff Pharmacist position. Some of the pharmacy directors who interviewed me spent more time looking at my extensive training rather than paying attention to their interviewee. One of the directors told me that I had accomplished much more in 2 years than he had done in 20 years. He politely said that I am almost too fancy in my poms and skirt suit to work in that department as if you are not supposed to look professional for interviews. I was aware that some of them violated some human resources (HR) codes by the things they said. I was in awe as I wondered how some of them ended up in their leadership roles, considering that they were out of line in their questions and comments. However, that was far from my problem at the time. I momentarily felt like a professional failure!

  I lived in a city and state supersaturated with pharmacists that you need almost ten years of work experience to get a job in a hospital setting. One day, out of frustration, I got into my car, put on what you may call "I have had enough" attitude, and drove out without a destination in mind. I came to a stop when I noticed a signboard for one of the company's that I had applied to a few months back, from whom I had received no response. I parked my car and walked in. I told the administrative assistant that was seated downstairs that I would like to speak with the pharmacy director, and she would not let me. She insisted that I go home and wait for an interview. The truth is that she was doing her job, but I would not bulge. I sat down and remained in the lobby, hoping to meet one of the pharmacy leaders as they come down for a break or lunch. It was not a hospital environment, so visitor restrictions were limited, and there was only one entrance elevator. I was attentive to the name badge of everyone that walked out of the elevator. I heard her calling someone and talking about me. First, I thought she was calling security (but I could care less), but she had called someone from HR to come down and explain the hiring process better to me since I seemed adamant. This pleasant HR lady came down and asked to see my CV. I handed it to her, and she asked, "why on earth would somebody with this CV not have a job?" and I answered, "you tell me." She beckoned me to go home and promised that someone would call me back the same day. Believing her, I drove straight home, and immediately I got home; while I was climbing the stairs headed to my bedroom, my phone rings and it was the pharmacy director. He interviewed me on the spot and subsequently invited me for an on-site interview the following day. The job was offered to me the same day at the end of the interview!

For some people, it may be harder to push through the limit when you are down in the valley of frustration, especially if you have had so many unfortunate outcomes and you have little or no strength left to push further. However, some others are more likely to push the limits in hopeless situations than they would in times when things are going as planned. Therefore, it is even harder to push the boundaries at the height of success because you have alternatives and may not want to waste your time at a dead end. Nonetheless, you should not only push your limits when frustrated or facing a colossal failure. I share both scenarios to help you realize that you can raise the bars in either situation. There are many times when people would like to tell you what you can and cannot do, especially when they think you are already comfortable. I want to believe that they probably speak from a place of concern and caution, and sometimes caution may be warranted. However, you should not expect your vision to be clear to someone who does not share in your foresight or passion. To that individual, you are making a reckless investment or pushing too hard. I am referring to the kind of zeal and persistence that happens when passion meets capability. Limits become redefined at that point, and you continue to raise the bars until you have maximized all potentials.

It is essential to recognize that comfort and comfort zones can become a stumbling block when pushing our limits. People can easily give several reasons why something or even a life-changing endeavor can never be possible. I have encountered few people who are in desperate need of jobs but are also unwilling to try opportunities outside their comfort zone. They stay in the same comfort zone for years and complain about their struggles even when prospects are calling elsewhere. It is different if there are some personal ties like taking care of aged parents or staying close to relatives. Outside these factors, the usual excuse is, "I don't want to leave here and start all over again." I have also heard excuses like, "I don't know anybody there."

I decided to complete a two-year post-doctoral pharmacy residency training after pharmacy school. Usually, successful candidates are offered positions through a matching process after the interviews. I was one of the lucky few selected for that year in my graduating class, and I was to complete my training in Utah. I was so excited and looking forward to the move from Houston, Texas, to Utah. Successful candidates were usually announced in class for recognition right before graduation. Then something remarkably interesting happened. I remember the whole experience as if it were yesterday. I was getting questions instead of congratulations. All I was getting from my classmates were comments like, "why are you going to Utah of all places?" I laughed within me because I could see beyond their marginalization. I was going to one of the best Health Systems in the nation, but everyone else around me at the time was too myopic to see that.

I am not sure if you know this, but most Africans (Nigerians mainly) prefer to live in places that feel close to home, and Houston, Texas, is one of those places. So, when I finished the training two years after, I went back to Houston because I missed the home connection. Upon my return, I was excited to see friends and acquaintances, except that, this time, I was no longer looking for a place that feels like my home country. I was looking for a well-rounded experience.

Almost one year after returning to the supposed "feel like home" city (my comfort zone), I accepted a job in Arizona and moved yet again! I may have just convinced some people, this time, that I have completely lost my mind. The initial reaction

I usually get when I tell anyone where I was moving to is, you are leaving Texas for Arizona?" Again, I will smile and say, "why not?" Then I will add, "I left Nigeria to come to the USA, not to come to Texas, so I will explore what this country has to offer, and that includes the 50 states in it. For the first two years, when some people call to check on me, the first question they ask is, "how are you doing in that desert?" What amazes me more is that Houston is also hot in the summer and very humid. By the way, I have nothing against these individuals; I am sure they are looking out for me. I am simply trying to make a point. We often allow what we call "comfort zone" to deny us the pleasure of other experiences we may have enjoyed if only we gave it a try. You may not always find life-transforming opportunities in your comfort zone, and you end up paying the price of the opportunity forgone. You have to take a leap of faith and expunge the bars of limitation.

We often don't attempt to work our way through some of these limitations because we fail to recognize what lies on the other side of the stumbling block before us. We are so focused on the barrier in front of us and magnify it so much that we fail to see what lies ahead even when it is conspicuously staring at us. When I see an opportunity that I like, I look beyond the barriers. The question I usually ask is, "how can I navigate through this barrier? Instead of asking, "why is this brick wall here and will I be able to go through it or around it?" In such cases, I focus my energy on the "how" instead of the "why."

Pushing the limits also entails that we take some time to rethink what matters most. For instance, the end of a professional career can be the beginning of a limitless opportunity in something you are passionate about but have failed to give it a try due to a daily job's demands. In this case, lateral growth can spring forth and thrive where an upward professional career ladder end. The net benefit, which includes enduring happiness, the profound joy that comes from the self-satisfaction of turning a passion into a career, and the possibility of a financial breakthrough, is nonquantifiable.

Chapter Highlight
When you give fear a position of power in your life, you unknowingly subscribe to failure.

The fear of failure is our greatest enemy when it comes to pushing the limits and breaking barriers. We often outline problems far better and faster than we can think of possible solutions. Consequently, we end up failing to try. I am not soliciting that you subscribe to risk-taking;

however, calculated risks are the actual test of your courage. You will never know the outcome until you try it yourself. Yes, I said "yourself" because your result may differ from that of the other people who have launched the same venture. Remember that you unknowingly subscribe to failure when you give fear a position of power in your life.

In the end, the actual limitations are the ones we set for ourselves. Growth and success are not only unidirectional and do not always have to follow an upward pattern. Growth and success are multifaceted. Hitting the finish line in one direction may mean the beginning of an endless opportunity in another course. It would help if you did not make conclusions about limitations until all potentials are explored and maximized.

Chapter 7

A Legacy that Lasts

Chapter Highlight
Great works are like magic; they take you to places your feet never imagined treading upon.

Sometimes we refer to legacy as something that happens at a specific time in our life and then stops. We look at it as snapshots in time, like a one-time act of benevolence. Others also consider it to be the amount of treasure left behind. The latter is close to one of the dictionary definitions of legacy. However, true legacy is not quantifiable. It goes beyond the amount of wealth and property left behind by the benefactors to be inherited. Consider some individuals, for instance, who handle their inheritance with so much disregard simply because they did not see the hard work that went into what they now possess. Consider some inherited real estate for whom the beneficiaries are oblivious of the struggle and arduous labor that went into acquiring the asset. The investments may yield profits and grow over time, but a true legacy is intangible. People work so hard to leave properties, wealth, and an impressive business empire behind yet, miss the most critical essence of their legacy. They forget, amidst the struggle to acquire tangible wealth, to leave a piece of themselves behind, which is necessary to outlive their presence when it is all said and done. A legacy that focuses on self-actualization, self-recognition, and self-gratification has lost the very essence of a true legacy. A true legacy is when people remember your life and selfless contributions before they think of your wealth. It is when people put your values first before your wealth. A true legacy is not about the end but about the entire journey, the works, sacrifices, energy, enthusiasm, commitment, and dedication that yields the results.

In the early nineties, we lost my maternal grandfather, who died at a celebrated age of one hundred and two years. I was a young teenager then, and in what you will call freshman year in high school. If you are from my country Nigeria or some other African country, you already understand what his funeral ceremony entails. It means we expect a crowd to show up for the funeral service and consequently more food and drinks for them. It also means an elaborate ceremony with more social and community groups to be entertained. People expect his corpse to be brought home in the best ambulance and casket. They hope to see dancers from different groups, a parade of cars, human traffic, and most notably, people will not cry much because he died at a considerably ripe age. My grandfather was a tall, handsome, well-built man, a strict disciplinarian but fun to be with (from a grandchild's perspective). I don't remember any funeral I have attended before his, but I sure remember the ones I attended after his.

My grandmother (who is now late; God bless her soul) needed company to distract her from the loss before and after the funeral celebration. So, my mom let me spend a few weeks with her. I was excited because staying with her means fewer errands, and which teenager will pass on that. I observed in complete disproof as some representatives of the different community groups came to outline what must be done for their respective groups as part of the funeral rites. However, I was perplexed by the immense favor that we received from people who mainly wanted to show that he was a great man.

Being a Christian, I watched out for the things that mattered most to me throughout his life and afterlife, and a few things stood out to me. My grandfather had two wives, and they both had children for him, yet he had so much peace in his home, much more than individuals with one wife. The love and respect shared amongst the two wives, and their children's unity was worthy of emulation.

Secondly, for someone who did not have an official wedding in the church due to polygamy, I was shocked at the number of reverend ministers and dignitaries who showed up to officiate his funeral service even though he was not a wealthy man. I emphasize this because he attended one of the traditional Orthodox churches. If you know the orthodox churches, you know that you are lucky to have the church secretary officiate your funeral ceremony if you fall short in any of the church ordinances. So being polygamous is already a significant strikeout! When my mom and his brothers went to invite one of the celebrated Reverend ministers of the church, he told them that he had so much respect for my grandfather's character and person and that it will be an honor to officiate his funeral service. Not only did he come, but there were three other ministers with him, and the burial ceremony became a revival and Christian crusade of some sort.

It has been long since he died, yet his name still commands respect among those fortunate enough to know him. A lasting legacy is not just for the wealthy and famous; popularity is extended to the poor and least prominent when we make the right impression on people.

It is crucial to think about your legacy each day of your life. Your legacy does not start at a certain age, as people may think. It is part of your life's purpose that you fulfill each day. It is a daily routine. People make the mistake of thinking that there are days set aside to make a difference, be nice, and reach out to people. Legacy is an action word and a continuous process. It should not have a future tense to it, neither should it have a past tense, except for when death knocks. More so, considering that we are all living a borrowed life, a tremendous personal CEO should live each day to make a difference as if it were the last day available to live.

When I think about leaving a legacy, I also remember a more recent experience. It was a beautiful afternoon. The day had started well; I woke up vibrant, energetic, enthusiastic, and optimistic. I quickly dressed up and went to work. There was a leadership meeting later that day. As usual, the agenda started with introductions of new leadership team members, followed by recognitions and presentations, and finally came the announcements. It was almost about closing time, and the CEO gets up to address the team as he is in the habit of doing. He will usually wrap up the meeting by thanking the team for their continued service and support. Everyone will usually leave in high spirits irrespective of any financial or operational challenges. Except that this time, the room was quiet, the atmosphere grew still, and you could almost hear the sound of a pin drop to the floor. No one moved from their seats, except for those who managed to walk up to him for a hug. People's eyes were wet; faces were red with wrinkles of disappointments and regrets. He has just announced his resignation after working as the CEO for a little under ten years. He was to leave in a few weeks. I have only been in this institution for barely a year, and I had the same impression of him. I could not utter a word. I sat back for a while. I was one of the last to leave the room as I wondered about the impact of this CEO's leadership on all of us. I looked around the room ten minutes after, and a few leaders were still there wiping their tears, unlike in previous meetings when people couldn't wait for it to be over so they can leave. This time, nobody wanted to go.

Amidst my disappointment about his imminent departure and worries about the future of the institution, I suddenly heard myself say, "this man has some good legacy." The first week I joined the health institution, I remember seeing him in the hallway, and he addressed me by my name. I expected him to ask, "what is that your name again?" I even had to think momentarily to remember his name, and he is the popular one! That was who he is. He knew everyone by name, and he was loved by all.

The legacy trail is like wearing a white dress or a white shirt in a crowd. First, everyone can easily spot you from the group; and whatever you do, whether positive or negative, is apparent. When you have a stain on the apparel, everyone sees it. When you leave a trail of goodwill, everyone also sees it. The scary aspect of life is that the people who look up to you and admire you (even the ones you don't know) see you all the time, including all your life's stains whether you wear white, yellow, or the darkest shade of green.

I used to be part of a certain Christian women's fellowship a few years ago, where I was allowed to share the word of God occasionally. While I know some of the women, I still struggled with remembering all their names. One day, I was discussing with a young lady in the fellowship after we had met in a choir meeting a few times, and she got to know me better. She is much younger and had a little girl. I inquired about her family, and she told me her story, for which I offered my advice. A few months later, I called her to let her know I was moving out of state, and she started telling me that I have been a source of inspiration to her. I did not think I had an inspiring encounter with her, so I asked her how? Everything she said had nothing to do with the time after I had come to know her more. She reminded me of a particular stand I had taken on a specific subject that represented her opinion when she had no voice. Her statements touched me but mainly reminded me to watch my steps.

Chapter Highlight
You have fewer regrets if you invest your time in things that matter most to you.

We often do have secret admirers who watch us closely and follow our footsteps every step all the way. When people look up to you as a mentor, your life is no longer just about you. You have to make sure that you are leading them right. Therefore, you have to be on the right path to lead others right.

Besides my grandfather's, I have been to some funeral ceremonies where you can see true legacy exemplified with powerful testimonials. I have also been to some, where there is nothing much to say, and the family members and friends are struggling to put words together in honor of the dead individual. Some will go as far as getting the help of a professional scriptwriter to put together a beautiful speech. You can even hear people wondering out loud in their murmurs and whispers and asking if the eulogy is for somebody else because they cannot remember witnessing any of the things shared. In this case, the person probably lived a self-centered life or a manipulative life at best, and so there is no good testimony to share. Unfortunately, at this point, the time is up, the pen is down, and the memory book is closed.

    I don't know if you have ever taken one of those personal life development surveys that attempt to identify the essential things in your life. The majority of the people in the different training sessions I have been to will usually choose within the categories of family, charity work, spending time with loved ones, healthy living, spiritual life development, etc. One popular item on everybody's list is spending time with family and loved ones, yet we have so many dysfunctional homes because priorities are often misplaced. If you are an actual CEO of your life and you fail to recognize, pay attention to, and invest your time in the very thing that is most important to you, then you are simply accumulating regrets for the later part of your life.

Have you heard about some life-changing stories where someone just recognized your family name and instantly favored you simply because someone from your family (father, grandfather, etc.) is unforgettably remarkable? I have realized that, even though we ought to work hard to accumulate wealth and riches, it is also essential to recognize that true legacies don't just exist in banks; they are living, breathing, moving beings. They result from someone else's inspiration, goodwill, motivation, guidance, encouragement, and relentless efforts to develop another life. Will your generation be fortunate enough to experience such unmerited favor attributable to your remarkable legacy? I hope that this chapter inspires you to be unforgettable in your distinctive way, no matter how rich or poor you are. Everyone can live a legacy. Legacy is not just for the affluent and flamboyant philanthropists. We all have something we can leave behind. God is perfect in His creation of man; in that He gave everyone something that somebody else does not have.

While you may be busy thinking about the tangible assets you are planning to leave behind for your loved ones, don't forget about the people out there who depend on your unquantifiable legacy to make it in life. Somebody's destiny is depending on the legacy you leave behind. Make a lasting positive impression of yourself.

LEADING ME

About the Author

Ndidi Precious Alino, PharmD, MS
Founder & Executive President of Diamond Sisters International (DSI) Elite Club

Dr. Alino is a creative nurturer and strategic leader with a deep sense of integrity, commitment, dedication, and drive to help others recognize their talent and maximize their potential. She is energetic, driven, and a forward thinker, full of ideas and not afraid to turn these ideas into reality.

She is originally from Imo State, Nigeria, raised in a family of seven. She moved to the United States in 2004 with her husband and two kids at the time. She eventually enrolled in a pharmacy program and earned her Doctor of Pharmacy degree from Texas Southern University Houston, Texas, in May of 2012. Upon completing the PharmD program, Dr. Alino moved to Salt Lake City, Utah, with her family. She completed a two-year post-doctoral pharmacy residency program while concurrently completing a Master of Science degree in Health-System Administration at the University of Utah.

Dr. Alino currently works as the Director of Pharmacy at Banner Ocotillo Medical Center (Banner Health's newest hospital). She was one of the first team of leaders who worked courageously and relentlessly to open this brand-new facility.

She was previously the Pharmacy Clinical Senior Manager at Banner Boswell Medical Center and the postgraduate Pharmacy Residency Program Director for five years. While serving in this role, she was appointed to serve as the Interim Director of Pharmacy for approximately seven months.

Dr. Alino enjoys a position that presents the opportunity to precept and mentor students and pharmacy residents and serves as an Adjunct Assistant Professor of Pharmacy Practice at Midwestern University Glendale College of Pharmacy since 2016. Dr. Alino occasionally serves as an Adjunct Faculty of Pharmacotherapeutics for

Advanced Practice Nurse Prescribers at Grand Canyon University.

In the larger society, Dr. Alino is committed to her faith (her source of strength), family, and the community. She served as one of the judges at the 2019 Miss Africa Arizona pageant. She is also a member of the African Diaspora Advisory Council of Arizona. Dr. Alino enjoys public speaking and shares a strong passion for mentoring, motivating, and empowering teenagers/youths and other women. She is the Executive President and founder of Diamond Sisters International Elite Club, a non-profit organization that motivates for greatness, discourages mediocrity, and empowers women and the youth for success.

She has been married to her husband Henry for 21 years. Their marriage is blessed with four children (3 teenagers and a toddler) that keep her busy. She enjoys singing and listening to music, reading inspirational books, writing, watching movies, spending time with family and friends, cooking, and trying out new recipes.

LEADING ME

Dr. Alino was my pharmacist preceptor in my advanced pharmacy practice rotations. Dr. Alino held a prestigious position in the hospital, was well known, and accomplished. Upon meeting her, I was not sure of what to expect. I was pleased as she was welcoming, compassionate, and relatable. One thing that resonated with me under Dr. Alino's guidance was her uniquely positive approach as a leader. For me, Dr. Alino is a true mentor. It was evident that she wanted to inspire higher thinking and encourage us to contemplate our role in the bigger picture of life.

When I think of leadership, Dr. Alino is someone who comes to mind immediately. She exudes confidence in her knowledge, which instills assurance and trust and contributes to her effectiveness as a leader and mentor. I knew that she had high standards for our work, which helped me strive to be the best. Under Dr. Alino's mentorship, I truly felt that what I was doing had a purpose. I completed one of the projects I am most proud of on my journey to becoming a pharmacist with Dr. Alino's advice and support.

~ Meranda Hirmiz, Pharm.D.

There is a famous quote that states, "if your actions inspire others to dream more, learn more, do more, and become more, you are a leader." These words could not be further from the truth when it comes to Precious. Precious is the type of leader who constantly challenges you to become a better pharmacist and person. Her ability never ceases to amaze me when it comes to growing others.

Precious is personable, dedicated, passionate, and creative. She motivates people to be their very best, inspires them to continue forming goals, helps them get back up when they fall, and if you lose sight, she will help guide you. When it comes to Precious, there is no limit. If you tell her there is, she will certainly prove you wrong.

~ **Cynthia Bui, PharmD, MBA**

There are only a handful of leaders who are genuinely interested in developing the gifts of others. Few leaders will help you to recognize and then leverage your strengths for upward mobility. Dr. Alino is this type of leader. Dr. Alino encourages the talents of those around her, helping them to see the possibilities in all the paths set before them. I know from first-hand experience having been one of Dr. Alino's direct reports. Dr. Alino's encouraging words combined with her "no excuse" motivational style have helped me discover the greatness that abounds within. Dr. Alino encourages those around her to think creatively, improvise and innovate. She then provides a platform unto which can exercise and revamp novel ideas.

Dr. Alino gives credit where credit is due in the true spirit of not just "sharing the spotlight" but allowing you to be in the spotlight. Understand that the foundations for success were already present within you. With a combination of her inspiratory words and euphemisms, you will be secure on the path of self and goal actualization.

~ Kristye J. Russell, PharmD, MS, BCPS

Precious Alino is a leader who inspires, mentors, and encourages those around her. She strives to bring the next generation to greater heights. Precious embraces change and calls for advancement where she sees mediocrity.

As a leader, she responds calmly under pressure rather than with a reactionary approach. Her confidence is immeasurable to those around her. She cultivates an environment of independence and motivation.

~ Maelee Brown, PharmD, BCPS

Also, By the Author

Knowledge

The path to knowledge is an eternal one.
Little by little, like drops of rain, a flood appears.
Unlike the rain, it dries not upon the appearance of the sun.
Neither does it come in season.
But little by little, it builds wonderous layers.
One upon another, though the eyes may not see it.

Like a child whose growth no one knows when it occurs.
Like a tree increases in height and thickness
Yet, like a tree in the springtime, more leaves and branches are seen day after day, but nobody has ever witnessed the exact time that this happens.
Everyone knows there is a difference but only sees it after it has occurred.

Just as a mother cannot say the particular time, her child grows.
Nor the planter aware of the precise moment the flowers sprout, so is the intellect oblivious of the exact time knowledge accumulates.
However, we know that the brain is in constant activity.

Some knowledge you have to work for, but others like grey hair just come to you.
You may not know how; you may not know when.
The path is an interesting one, and everyone is welcome to its cause.
Yet all must tread with caution because there are two ends to its use.

~ *First written in 2010 and shared on the Lozenge Magazine (a magazine of the African Pharmacy Students Association) at Texas Southern University.*

Momentum: For the College Student

When an object is in motion, it is said to have momentum. Momentum is a vector, and as such, has size (magnitude) and direction, according to "College Physics." I also learned in the same class that momentum is a conserved quantity, which means that several factors within a system might be interacting with each other but not being influenced by forces from outside the system. An object with momentum is on the move and usually very difficult to bring to a halt. To a physics student, momentum is basically defined by the equation; $P = m * v$; where p = size of the momentum, m= mass of the object, and v = object's velocity. If we can translate this concept to personal ability and success, momentum, therefore, means inner strength (Si) and can be defined by the equation; $Si = determination \times courage + dedication$ (determination multiplied by courage plus dedication). It is clear from the equation that you can only have high momentum if the variables on the equation's right side are increasing.

If you notice, I did not include brilliance in the equation above because brilliance alone does not yield success. Brilliance is an added advantage when it comes naturally. Nonetheless, when there is determination working in conjunction with dedication through self-discipline, brilliance is undermined. Determination is the fundamental factor, which someone can exponentially increase with courage. However, determination and courage are great for a start, but success stories are not without dedication. Dedication is necessary to sustain the initial result of determination and courage.

Highlight
Dedication is the hope of ambition, but self-discipline is the propelling force that brings growth and sustains your dream.

When in college, momentum (Si) is something you want to accumulate in excess. Life is full of surprises, you may be disappointed with some exams' outcome, but that is just an aspect of life's surprises. Nevertheless, a clear understanding of your destination helps you remain encouraged and stay on the right track. It might not be your favorite track or path, but if you know the distance that needs to be covered and the direction to follow, you will undoubtedly get to your destination. Just as we take different routes every day to get to our respective destinations, there are other learning/study methods one can explore to produce the desired result. Be it as it may, I am inclined to mention here that there are NO SHORTCUTS to success.

For some students, it has always been a smooth ride, no flat tires (any other kind of misfortunes) along the way, only A's and occasional B's. Meanwhile, for some other students, life has been full of flat tires with several complications. It does not necessarily mean that those that have it smooth are better; that's just how life is sometimes. You may have failed one class or received a disappointing grade at some point. Do you literally leave your car on the road and go home each time you get a flat tire? I don't think you answered yes to that question. The ideal thing is always to carry a spare tire, use it to fix the car, and then continue the journey. The same goes for academics, fix the problem rather than let it put you to a fix. As a student, having a lot of momentum requires that you load up on inner strength (your spare tire).

The first time I heard about momentum in Physics class, I considered it one of those numerous topics that I must understand to pass the course. I defined it as a physicist would. Little did I know that it will come to mean so much more. It is something I long to possess each day, and it is something I watch as I would my gasoline gauge (knowing when I need a refill, so I don't entirely run out). By the way, did I mention that you, too, need to watch your meter and get occasional refills? You can check your refill status on your "view Grade" tab. Trust me; a bad grade is the best determinant of your inner strength.

In the spirit of MOMENTUM, let's be on the move. Don't be stagnant; push hard on the accelerator but apply brakes when necessary. Never decelerate in the middle of the freeway; it is precarious. FORWARD EVER, BACKWARD NEVER!!!! Therefore, what is your P-value? If P = size of your momentum.

Are you ready to lead YOU?

Hopefully this book has inspired you to lead the many different aspects of your life like a seasoned life CEO.

For personal inquiries and to share your ideas and insights please email the author at:

DrP@credablemindset.com

To learn more about the author's speaking engagement and life coaching consulting services please visit:

www.credablemindset.com

LEADING ME

www.ingramcontent.com/pod-product-compliance
Lightning Source LLC
Chambersburg PA
CBHW031149160426
43193CB00008B/306